Mark Twain

WHO
WROTE
THAT?

Mark Twain

Liz Sonneborn

Foreword by
Kyle Zimmer

CHELSEA HOUSE
PUBLISHERS

An imprint of Infobase Publishing

Mark Twain

Copyright © 2011 by Infobase Publishing

Chelsea House
An imprint of Infobase Publishing
132 West 31st Street
New York, NY 10001

Library of Congress Cataloging-in-Publication Data
Sonneborn, Liz.
  Mark Twain / Liz Sonneborn.
  p. cm. — (Who wrote that?)
  Includes bibliographical references and index.
  ISBN 978-1-60413-728-6 (hardcover)
  1. Twain, Mark, 1835–1910—Juvenile literature. 2. Authors, American—19th century—Biography—Juvenile literature. 3. Children's stories—Authorship—Juvenile literature. I. Title. II. Series.
  PS1331.S65 2010
  818'.409—dc22
  [B]   2010006601

Chelsea House books are available at special discounts when purchased in bulk quantities for business, associations, institutions, or sales promotions. Please call our Special Sales Department in New York at (212) 967-8800 or (800) 322-8755.

You can find Chelsea House on the World Wide Web at http://www.chelseahouse.com.

Text design by Keith Trego
Cover design by Alicia Post
Composition by EJB Publishing Services
Cover printed by Bang Printing, Brainerd, MN
Book printed and bound by Bang Printing, Brainerd, MN
Date printed: November 2010
Printed in the United States of America

10 9 8 7 6 5 4 3 2 1

This book is printed on acid-free paper.

All links and Web addresses were checked and verified to be correct at the time of publication. Because of the dynamic nature of the Web, some addresses and links may have changed since publication and may no longer be valid.

Table of Contents

FOREWORD BY
KYLE ZIMMER
PRESIDENT, FIRST BOOK

HUMANITY IS POWERED by stories. From our earliest days as thinking beings, we employed every available tool to tell each other stories. We danced, drew pictures on the walls of our caves, spoke, and sang. All of this extraordinary effort was designed to entertain, recount the news of the day, explain natural occurrences—and then gradually to build religious and cultural traditions and establish the common bonds and continuity that eventually formed civilizations. Stories are the most powerful force in the universe; they are the primary element that has distinguished our evolutionary path.

Our love of the story has not diminished with time. Enormous segments of societies are devoted to the art of storytelling. Book sales in the United States alone topped $24 billion in 2006; movie studios spend fortunes to create and promote stories; and the news industry is more pervasive in its presence than ever before.

There is no mystery to our fascination. Great stories are magic. They can introduce us to new cultures, or remind us of the nobility and failures of our own, inspire us to greatness or scare us to death; but above all, stories provide human insight on a level that is unavailable through any other source. In fact, stories connect each of us to the rest of humanity not just in our own time, but also throughout history.

This special magic of books is the greatest treasure that we can hand down from generation to generation. In fact, that spark in a child that comes from books became the motivation for the creation of my organization, First Book, a national literacy program with a simple mission: to provide new books to the most disadvantaged children. At present, First Book has been at work in hundreds of communities for over a decade. Every year children in need receive millions of books through our organization and millions more are provided through dedicated literacy institutions across the United States and around the world. In addition, groups of people dedicate themselves tirelessly to working with children to share reading and stories in every imaginable setting from schools to the streets. Of course, this Herculean effort serves many important goals. Literacy translates to productivity and employability in life and many other valid and even essential elements. But at the heart of this movement are people who love stories, love to read, and want desperately to ensure that no one misses the wonderful possibilities that reading provides.

When thinking about the importance of books, there is an overwhelming urge to cite the literary devotion of great minds. Some have written of the magnitude of the importance of literature. Amy Lowell, an American poet, captured the concept when she said, "Books are more than books. They are the life, the very heart and core of ages past, the reason why men lived and worked and died, the essence and quintessence of their lives." Others have spoken of their personal obsession with books, as in Thomas Jefferson's simple statement: "I live for books." But more compelling, perhaps, is the almost instinctive excitement in children for books and stories.

Throughout my years at First Book, I have heard truly extraordinary stories about the power of books in the lives of children. In one case, a homeless child, who had been bounced from one location to another, later resurfaced—and the only possession that he had fought to keep was the book he was given as part of a First Book distribution months earlier. More recently, I met a child who, upon receiving the book he wanted, flashed a big smile and said, "This is my big chance!" These snapshots reveal the true power of books and stories to give hope and change lives.

As these children grow up and continue to develop their love of reading, they will owe a profound debt to those volunteers who reached out to them—a debt that they may repay by reaching out to spark the next generation of readers. But there is a greater debt owed by all of us—a debt to the storytellers, the authors, who have bound us together, inspired our leaders, fueled our civilizations, and helped us put our children to sleep with their heads full of images and ideas.

WHO WROTE THAT? is a series of books dedicated to introducing us to a few of these incredible individuals. While we have almost always honored stories, we have not uniformly honored storytellers. In fact, some of the most important authors have toiled in complete obscurity throughout their lives or have been openly persecuted for the uncomfortable truths that they have laid before us. When confronted with the magnitude of their written work or perhaps the daily grind of our own, we can forget that writers are people. They struggle through the same daily indignities and dental appointments, and they experience the intense joy and bottomless despair that many of us do. Yet somehow they rise above it all to deliver a powerful thread that connects us all. It is a rare honor to have the opportunity that these books provide to share the lives of these extraordinary people. Enjoy.

The great American author Mark Twain, born Samuel Langhorne Clemens, stands in front of his childhood home in Hannibal, Missouri, on his last visit to his hometown in May 1902.

1

A Visit Home

IN LATE MAY 1902, a young man named Robertus Love was on a train en route for Missouri. A reporter for the *St. Louis Post-Dispatch*, Love was after a hot story. He had heard that the author Mark Twain, then one of the most famous people in the United States, was aboard.

Love approached a baggage carrier and asked him if Twain was really on the train. When the porter said he was, Love handed him a card printed with his name and position. "Will you carry my card into Mr. Clemens' drawing room?"[1] Love asked. The porter became confused. "Into who?" he replied. "Say, I thought you wanted to see Mr. Twain."[2] Love then explained that Mr. Clemens and Mr. Twain were in fact one and the same. "Mr. Clemens is a writer," he told the porter, "a man who writes funny books, and he uses Mark Twain when he writes."[3]

Mark Twain, however, was more than just a writer of funny books. Over his long career, he became the best known and perhaps most beloved writer in the country. Twain's books were wildly popular not only in the United States, but around the world. He was equally famous as a performer on the lecture circuit. Twain had toured the globe, offering his witty speeches to audiences of all nationalities. Given Twain's renown, it was hardly surprising that Love wanted to talk with him. Everywhere Twain went, journalists sought him out, eager to record his thoughts on the important events of the day. Twain had a knack for coming up with clever off-the-cuff remarks that cut to the core of an issue and, even more important from the reporter's perspective, made for copy newspaper buyers loved to read.

A SENSATION IN ST. LOUIS

After receiving Love's card, Twain graciously invited Love to his quarters for breakfast. The great writer, then 66 years old, was finding it hard to get a good night's sleep on the train. He had been aboard for days, traveling from his home in New York City to the town of Columbia, Missouri, where he was to be awarded an honorary doctorate of law from the University of Missouri.

Twain was eager to visit the city of St. Louis during a brief stopover. He told Love he had not truly seen St. Louis since 1861. He did make trips there a few times on lecture tours, but they had not been real visits. "In fact, I merely flitted past," Twain said. "I flit into many cities and flit out. . . . I'm a flitter and have been one for a good many years."[4]

Twain agreed to let Love accompany him so the reporter could record his visit to St. Louis. Arriving in the morning of May 29, Twain and his young friend were met at the train station by Twain's cousin James Ross Clemens, a well-respected pediatrician. They walked together to Planters' Hotel, with Twain attracting a swarm of well-wishers, as he did wherever he traveled. As a reporter for the *St. Louis Star* wrote, "Mark, genial, affable, continuously saying whimsical things, took the adulation with quaint dignity."[5]

In the hotel lobby, Twain held court for a gathering of new and old acquaintances. He told stories about growing up in Missouri and reminisced with friends he had not seen in years. Among them was Horace Bixby, who long ago had trained young Samuel Clemens to pilot a steamboat up and down the great Mississippi River. Clemens, writing as Mark Twain, would later immortalize the experience in his popular book *Life on the Mississippi* (1883).

By midday, Twain managed to break away from his adoring audience and pay a visit to the city's Merchants Exchange. There, he received the kind of reception he had come to expect wherever he went. According to the *St. Louis Star*, "Recognition was instant on all sides, and handclapping broke into cheers. Soon Mr. Clemens was surrounded by a mass of yelling men, and shouts for a speech went up on every hand."[6] He was guided to a rostrum, and the crowd immediately closed in around him, with all eager to hear every word he had to say. Twain gave a short speech in which he declared, "I am glad to be back in Missouri, the State that gave me birth, and trusted me for it, never knowing how I would pay her back."[7]

After shaking dozens of hands, Twain left the Exchange, grabbed a quick lunch, and made his way back to the train station, with reporter Robertus Love in tow.

SURPRISING HANNIBAL

Just a few hours after he arrived, Twain flitted out of St. Louis for a spur-of-the-moment trip to the small city of Hannibal. The impulsive decision to see Hannibal was a sentimental one. It was the place he had spent most of his boyhood. But Hannibal was more than Twain's hometown. It was also the inspiration for some of his most beloved books, including *The Adventures of Tom Sawyer* (1876) and its sequel, *Adventures of Huckleberry Finn* (1884). Twain had been in Hannibal 12 years earlier to bury his mother, but he had left just after the funeral. This time, he wanted to spend a few days there. Twain figured it might be his last chance to see the town that he had left 50 years earlier to go off in search of his own adventures.

Twain had not sent word ahead that he was coming to Hannibal. But almost as soon as he stepped off the train, dozens of passersby stopped in their tracks and rushed to greet him. The citizens of Hannibal had not seen Twain for many years, but as in everywhere else in the United States, his distinctive face was well known from published photographs. Twain had large blue eyes and a head of shaggy hair colored silvery white with a mustache to match. He favored well-tailored suits and always seemed to have a big black cigar poised in the side of his mouth.

He walked a block to the Windsor Hotel, where he asked for a room. The desk clerk immediately recognized his guest. "Mr. Clemens," he said, "I was born close to your birthplace at Florida, [Missouri,] and have been in the house where you were born, often." Twain, as always, was quick with a wry response: "I was not born often—only once, but I'm glad to see you, all the same."[8]

Much to the townspeople's distress, Twain, only 10 minutes after arriving in Hannibal, holed himself up in his room for the night. News that Twain was in Hannibal spread throughout the city of 12,000 and soon hordes were descending on the Windsor Hotel. According to Robertus Love, "Old and young and middle-aged, they arrived afoot, by street car, and in carriages. To each the hotel clerk gave the disappointing information that the guest had retired and must not be disturbed."[9]

LOOKING UP OLD FRIENDS

After a long night's rest, Twain emerged from his hotel room, ready to face the citizens of Hannibal. His first day in town was busy, with nearly everyone trying to get a few minutes of Twain's time and attention. In the hotel lobby,

Did you know...

Mark Twain's famous character Huckleberry Finn was based on a real person—his boyhood friend Tom Blankenship. Tom's alcoholic father barely provided food or clothing for Tom. Other adults shunned the filthy, scrawny boy and forbade their children to play with him, which, as Twain later recalled, had the effect of making Tom all the more popular with his peers. Twain envied Tom's independence, which he claimed made Tom the happiest person in all of Hannibal.

The home of Laura Hawkins, whom Samuel Clemens loved and later immortalized as the character Becky Thatcher in his novel **The Adventures of Tom Sawyer.**

he encountered a throng of admirers, including a few childhood playmates. He cheerfully greeted his old friend Edwin Pierce with, "How are you doing, Eddie?" Acknowledging that they were now both old men, Pierce responded, "Like yourself, Sam, like a cow's tail going down."[10]

Twain wandered through the town, followed by a crowd of fans. He made a point of visiting 206 Hill Street, the house in which he had grown up. The dingy little building seemed less impressive in person than it had been in his memories. Twain said, "It seems to have grown smaller. A boy's home is a mighty big place to him. Why, I believe that if I should come back here ten years hence it would be no bigger than a bird house."[11]

Helen Garth, a wealthy widow of an old friend, offered Twain a carriage ride. They traveled to the city's cemetery, where he saw the graves of his parents and his brothers, Henry and Orion. Twain then headed to the First Presbyterian Church, which he had attended as a child with his mother. Asked to speak, he talked about how overwhelmed he was by his reception in Hannibal:

> The expressions in their face and the hand grasps and the words that have greeted me have been something more than friendship, and that something is affection, the proudest thing an old man may possess, and in granting me that this city of my earliest time has stirred me with the profoundest compliment.[12]

Hannibal's excitement over Twain's visit was also clear in peculiar changes in the clothing worn by the city's young people. Suddenly, children born many decades after Twain had left Hannibal were dressing up like his famous characters based on his childhood friends. Often to their annoyance, older people in town were also being named as models for Twain's creations. Trying to find inspirations for Becky Thatcher, the pretty young girl in *Tom Sawyer*, became an especially popular new pastime in Hannibal. One reporter said that no fewer than 18 supposed first sweethearts of Twain had been discovered since he arrived. During his visit, Twain did have a chance to reminisce with the real Becky Thatcher: Helen Garth had invited Twain and his first girlfriend, Laura Hawkins, to a dinner at her house.

A FOND FAREWELL

Another highlight of his trip was attending the graduation ceremony for the Hannibal High School. In a move the school perhaps came to regret, it invited Twain to hand out the diplomas. Twain fanned out the documents, all carefully rolled and bound in blue and red ribbons, and invited the graduates to grab whichever one they wanted. "Take one, take a good one," he said. "Now, don't take two, but be sure and get a good one."[13] The students gleefully snatched the diplomas without any care to whose name was on them. True to Twain's reputation as America's greatest humorist, he turned a solemn graduation into a scene of mayhem, with the young people giggling and laughing as they traded diplomas, eventually returning each one to its rightful owner.

For the people of Hannibal, the most anticipated moment of Twain's visit was his reception at the Labinnah Club. Labinnah (Hannibal spelled backward) was the finest social club in the city. At its invitation, Twain addressed the club, with some 500 guests in attendance. The excited audience members, dressed in their finest gowns and suits, were all prepared to laugh long and hard at Twain's legendary wit. Instead, they were stunned when Twain, as he took the podium, began to weep. His shoulders heaving with the many emotions unleashed by his visit, he was finally able to choke out, "I realize that this must be my last visit to Hannibal and in bidding you hail [hello] I also bid you farewell."[14]

These were not the only tears Twain shed on his trip. The next day, he set out in a carriage with his old friend John Briggs to see the places where they had played as boys. Overlooking the Mississippi, Twain said to his companion, "John, that is the prettiest sight I ever saw. There is the place by the island where we used to swim. . . . 'Twas fifty years ago, John, and yet it seems as yesterday."[15] At the end of their nostalgic journey, the two men, with moistened eyes, shook hands. "Good-bye, John," Twain said. "If we never meet again here, I'll try to meet you on the other side."[16]

AN AMERICAN LEGEND

On the morning of Tuesday, June 3, Mark Twain's sentimental trip to Hannibal came to an end. Surrounded by a crowd of friends and fans, he wandered through its downtown one last time before boarding the train that would take him on to Columbia. When a reporter asked Twain if he had enjoyed his time in Hannibal, he replied, "This visit of mine back to the scene of my boyhood has been one of the happy events of my life."[17]

Twain's prediction that he would never again see Hannibal was correct. But he did try to revisit the town in his writing. Twain started a manuscript about an elderly Tom Sawyer and Huck Finn called *Fifty Years Later*, but he never managed to finish it. Twain could physically visit the town for a few days, but emotionally and mentally, he now seemed unable to return to the world he left so many years before. Perhaps, 50 years after he first left Hannibal, there was just too much distance between the young Samuel Clemens and the old Mark Twain.

Another prediction Twain made during his trip to Hannibal—that he would soon be dead—proved not as accurate. The famed author would live another eight years, during which his celebrity would only grow. In fact, now 100 years after his death, Twain's stature as a great author is as secure as it was in his own time. He remains just as beloved today for his wit, his wisdom, and his unparalleled contribution to American literature.

*The little cabin in Florida, Missouri, where Samuel Langhorne Clemens—
who would become famous the world over as Mark Twain—was born on
November 30, 1835.*

2

Growing Up

ON THE NIGHT of November 30, 1835, Samuel Langhorne Clemens was born in a little cabin in Florida, Missouri. He was the sixth of seven children born to Jane and John Clemens. Arriving two months premature, Sam was so sickly that his parents feared he might not survive. But, to the family's surprise and delight, Sam grew healthy and hardy. The baby was soon sporting a head of red hair, just like his mother.

When Sam was three, the Clemens family decided to leave Florida. The small village seemed like a dead end, especially to Sam's father. John Clemens had come from a respected family in Virginia and was determined to make a success of himself.

He bet that his future lay in Hannibal, a newly established settlement about 35 miles (56.3 kilometers) to the southeast of Florida. Although it was home to only about 1,000 people, Hannibal seemed poised to grow.

When the Clemens family moved to Hannibal, the United States included only 24 states, and Missouri was situated on what was then the nation's western border. The town of Hannibal was located on the Mississippi River, which was the key to its promise. On this mighty river, dozens of steamboats carrying passengers and goods passed by Hannibal every day. John Clemens was sure that the river trade would turn Hannibal into a prosperous city where his family could thrive.

A MISSOURI BOYHOOD

After the family moved into a modest house, John Clemens set about making his mark in their new town. He established a hotel called the Virginia House, but he had to shut its doors when Hannibal failed to attract as many visitors as he had expected. Clemens then decided to try his luck with a dry goods store. This venture also failed, leaving Clemens in debt. He managed to make a little money serving as a justice of the peace, but the family was never again on a firm financial footing. Eventually, they had to sell their house and furniture and move into a small apartment above a drugstore. His mother worked as a cook for the store's owner to pay the rent.

John Clemens was a failure not only as a provider, but also as a father. He was cold and stern toward his children and never showed anyone in the family much affection. As Sam later recalled, "My father and I were always on the most distant terms when I was a boy—a sort of armed neutrality, so to speak."[1] Sam got along much better with

At right, the childhood home of Samuel Clemens in Hannibal, Missouri. The future author's father believed the trade along the nearby Mississippi River would help his growing family thrive in Hannibal.

his mother. In addition to red hair, he shared with her a love of music, witty conversation, and storytelling. "My mother [was] very much alive, fond of excitement, fond of novelties, fond of anything going that was of a sort proper for members of the church to indulge in,"[2] Sam once wrote. As much as he enjoyed his mother's spirit of fun, Sam never warmed to her love of churchgoing. He disliked hearing the kinds of sermons that tried to fill him with guilt and shame, and he often snuck out of the Bible classes his mother forced him to attend.

Sam also had little enthusiasm for school. He was at best a mediocre student who was prone to playing hooky. The countryside near Hannibal was much more attractive to him than the classroom. Sam loved to play with his friends in nearby forests and go swimming in the Mississippi. Sometimes, they spent entire days on an island in the great river, far from their parents and the grown-up world. There, Sam could let his imagination go wild. He pretended to be a pirate or a lion tamer or Robin Hood. Probably influenced by tales of the California Gold Rush that began in 1848, he and his pals often went in search of buried treasure.

UNCLE DAN'L'S CABIN

From the ages of 8 to 12, Sam spent his summers on the farm of his uncle, John Quarles. His parents probably sent Sam away to save a little money, but he had no objections. The farm, located near Florida, offered many entertainments for a boy. It was always full of cats and cousins to play with. But even better to Sam was the open invitation he had to visit Uncle Dan'l. Despite his name, he was not

Did you know...

As a boy, Samuel Clemens shared his mother's love of cats. When he grew up, no matter where he lived, he liked to have at least a few cats in his household. He enjoyed giving them amusing names, such as Satan for a favorite black cat and Sin for her little kitten. As an older man, he once found himself catless while staying at a summer home. He soon remedied the situation by arranging with a neighbor to rent a few barn kittens, which he returned once the summer was over.

a relative of Sam. He was one of several African-American slaves owned by Sam's actual Uncle John. In the kitchen of Uncle Dan'l's little cabin, Sam sat for hours while the slave told wonderful stories about ghosts, witches, and animals that could talk. Uncle Dan'l also shared other less whimsical tales. He told Sam about black families that had been broken up when white slave owners decided to sell some of their slaves. He also recounted stories of escapes and near escapes by slaves desperate to live as free people.

Sam never forgot Uncle Dan'l and his tales. He was impressed not just by the stories themselves but also by how he told them. Uncle Dan'l's rich use of language, passed down by slave storytellers from generation to generation, would have a great impact on the boy's later career as a writer.

Despite his affection for Uncle Dan'l, young Sam did not think that slavery was wrong or evil. Like most white people in Missouri at the time, he regarded slavery as a natural state of affairs, not a gross violation of justice and decency. Sam's church helped reinforce this idea. Although other churches, particularly Quaker churches and other evangelical Christians, condemned slavery and sought to abolish it, many ministers routinely held up slavery in the Bible as proof that God himself approved of the institution. As Sam later explained, he was taught to view slavery as "a holy thing."[3]

Still, it was impossible even for a young boy to close his eyes completely to the horrors of the lives of slaves. He once watched as his father beat the family's only slave, a woman named Jennie, for talking back to Sam's mother. Sam cried when John Clemens finally sent Jennie down the Mississippi to be auctioned off in the slave markets of New Orleans, Louisiana—a fate many slaves felt was worse than death.

Many years later, Sam recorded a shocking event he had witnessed as a child:

> When I was ten years old I saw a man fling a lump of iron-ore at a slave-man in anger, for merely doing something awkwardly—as if that were a crime. It bounded from the man's skull, and the man fell and never spoke again. He was dead in an hour. . . . Nobody in the village approved of that murder, but of course no one said much about it.[4]

LEARNING THE PRINTING TRADE

After years of struggling to make ends meet, John Clemens was finally close to establishing a well-paying career in 1847. He was the lead candidate in an election for county court clerk, a post that offered a substantial salary. While campaigning, Clemens was caught in a sleet storm. Soon after he returned home, wet and exhausted, he developed pneumonia and died, leaving the Clemens children without a father and the family without a breadwinner.

The family had to turn to Sam's oldest brother, Orion, for help. Years before, to ease their financial worries, his parents had taken Orion out of school and sent him to St. Louis, where he learned to work as a printer. With John's death, Orion became the head of the family. He sent whatever money he could home to Hannibal, but it was never enough. Sam's mother took in boarders. His sister Pamela taught piano, and Sam worked odd jobs. Finally, three years after his father's death, his mother decided that Sam had to leave school for good and follow his brother into the printing trade. At 13, he became an apprentice printer working for the *Missouri Courier*. There, the editor trained Sam to be a typesetter. At the time, newspapers were printed using pieces of metal with raised letters and words that were covered with ink and then pressed onto paper using a printing press. Setting the type by hand was a hard job. A typesetter had to be both accurate and fast if the paper were to come out on time.

A few years later, Sam went to work for the *Hannibal Journal*, a newspaper run by Orion. Sam grew frustrated with his scatterbrained brother, who proved just as inept at making a living as his father had been. Orion had promised to give Sam a salary of three and a half dollars each week. In the two years Sam worked for him, he never saw a penny.

But at the *Journal*, Sam learned something valuable: He liked to write and was good at it. Much of what was printed in small newspapers at that time were articles copied from larger papers and magazines. As a printer, Sam read constantly and critically. He quickly came to the conclusion that he could write as well, if not better, than journalists working for high-toned periodicals. For the *Journal*, Sam began writing poems and humorous sketches under funny names, such as W. Epaminondas Adrastus Blab. Readers liked his work, and his pieces soon caught the eye of editors at other newspapers. One sketch from 1852 titled "The Dandy Frightening the Squatter" was reprinted in a paper in Boston, Massachusetts, a sophisticated eastern city as far away culturally as it was geographically from Sam's little western town.

One early story of Sam's was not quite as well received. While his brother was out of town, Sam wrote a savage little piece making fun of the editor of a rival paper for trying to kill himself after a romantic breakup. The editor stormed into the *Journal* office, threatening to kill Sam, before seeing that he was hardly older than a boy.

HEADING EAST

In the spring of 1853, Sam Clemens, then 17, was desperate to leave home. He was sick of working for his brother and his failing newspaper. He was also tired of Hannibal. The town was just too small to hold such an ambitious young man.

After promising never to take up drinking or gambling, he convinced his mother to allow him to move to St. Louis, where his sister Pamela lived. For a few months, he set type at the *St. Louis Evening News*. Even though St. Louis was the largest city in Missouri, it was still not big enough for Clemens. In August, he boarded a train for the first time and ran away to New York City.

Clemens was lured to New York in part because it was hosting the World's Fair, a spectacle featuring exhibitions from around the globe. But he also wanted to test himself and his talents in a large eastern city. At the time, Americans from the western states often felt unsophisticated in comparison to easterners. For Clemens, finding success in New York was a far more exciting prize than finding success in Hannibal could ever be.

After getting a job in a print shop, Clemens began writing letters home about his impressions of big city life. Orion published his colorful descriptions in the *Hannibal Journal*. Clemens worked hard to make his correspondence as intriguing and informative as possible. As he made clear in a note to his sister, he was disappointed by how much his family's letter-writing skills fell short of his own: "I have received one or two letters from home, but they are not written as they should be; and [I] know no more about what is going on there than the man in the moon. One only has to leave home to learn how to write an interesting [letter]."[5]

A NEW DIRECTION

Clemens's natural restlessness kept him from staying in New York City for long. A few months after arriving, he moved to Philadelphia, Pennsylvania, where he set type for the *Philadelphia Inquirer*. While there, he made a point of visiting the grave of one of the nation's great Founding Fathers, Benjamin Franklin. Clemens wrote enthusiastically about the visit in a letter to Orion. The two brothers felt a kinship with Franklin, who, like them, had started his career in the printing trade. Clemens also described an aspect of Philadelphia he did not care for—the presence of a large population of free African Americans, who, in his eyes, were not properly subservient to whites. Using the vulgar terminology common in slave states, he wrote, "I reckon I had better black my face for in these Eastern States n-----s are considerably better than white people."[6]

In 1854, Clemens moved to Washington, D.C., but after just a few months, he decided to return to the West. In the East, the high cost of living and the competition for jobs in the printing industry made it almost impossible for Clemens to get by. Reluctantly, he headed to Keokuk, Iowa, where his mother, his brothers Henry and Orion, and Orion's new wife now lived. Once again, Clemens went to work for Orion, and once again, he became angry at Orion's refusal to pay him. He soon left Iowa and began wandering from city to city. He spent time in first St. Louis; then Chicago, Illinois; and then Cincinnati, Ohio.

Unable to settle down in one city or one job, Clemens came up with a foolhardy scheme to strike it rich. He decided to take a riverboat called the *Paul Jones* to New Orleans. From its port, he planned to board another ship bound for Brazil. There, he would start a business trading in coca plants, which provided an ingredient then used in medicines. Despite his conviction that coca would make him a fortune, Clemens never made it to Brazil. Instead, aboard the *Paul Jones*, he discovered a new profession and ushered in one of the happiest periods of his life.

The Mississippi, *a watercolor painting by Hippolyte Sebron, now located in a museum in Blerancourt, France. A young Samuel Clemens learned to pilot riverboats like the one seen here.*

3

A Writer in the West

SINCE CHILDHOOD, SAMUEL Clemens had dreamed of becoming a riverboat pilot. In Hannibal, the pilots who helmed the boats that filled the Mississippi were considered celebrities. The job not only gave pilots social standing, but it also delivered a sizable paycheck—something that Clemens longed for, given his family's history of financial trouble.

While aboard the *Paul Jones*, Clemens approached pilot Horace Bixby with a proposal. He asked to become Bixby's apprentice. Bixby agreed, but only after negotiating a high price for teaching Clemens the intricacies of riverboat piloting. Clemens had to pay Bixby $500 (the equivalent of about

$12,000 in today's dollars)—half up front, half from his wages once he became a working pilot. After persuading his brother-in-law to lend him $250, Clemens began his training.

RIVERBOAT DAYS

From Bixby, Clemens slowly began to learn the Mississippi River. It was not easy. The Mississippi stretched 1,200 miles (1,931.2 km) from St. Louis to New Orleans. To pilot a boat competently, he had to memorize every bend on both sides of the river. He later wrote that the task was like memorizing both testaments of the Bible and having to "recite them glibly, forward or backward, or begin at random anywhere in the book and recite both ways and never trip or make a mistake."[1] But for Clemens, getting to truly know the Mississippi was as delightful as it was challenging. As the future author later explained:

> The face of the water, in time, became a wonderful book—a book that was a dead language to the uneducated passenger, but which told its mind to me without reserve, delivering its most cherished secrets as clearly as if it uttered them with a voice. And it was not a book to be read once and thrown aside, for it had a new story to tell every day.[2]

In the decades to come, Clemens recalled his four years on the river as a golden time. But he also experienced one of the greatest tragedies of his life during this same period. In early 1858, Orion Clemens closed his failed printing business. Henry Clemens had been working there, so he was also out of a job. Sam decided to help his little brother by getting him a job as a clerk on the *Pennsylvania*, the riverboat on which he was a cub pilot. In New Orleans, Sam

The riverboat pilot's license of Samuel Clemens. His pen name, Mark Twain, was inspired by the time he spent as a pilot along the Mississippi River, which served as a backdrop in many of his most famous works.

Clemens, however, was soon transferred to another boat, the *A.T. Lacey*, after he got into a fight with the chief pilot of the *Pennsylvania*. The Clemens brothers were separated, but they made plans to meet at their sister's house in St. Louis once their respective boats had made the trip upriver. The *Pennsylvania* went first, followed two days later by the *A.T. Lacey*.

During the trip, Sam Clemens heard someone on the shore shouting. The voice warned that off the coast of Memphis, Tennessee, the boilers in the *Pennsylvania* had exploded. Clemens was frantic until he got his hands on a newspaper that listed Henry as one of the survivors. A second newspaper, however, delivered grim news. While trying to help those injured by the first explosion, Henry was badly burned by another explosion. Clemens found Henry in a Memphis hospital and sat with him until he died a painful death. Clemens, overcome with grief and guilt, forever blamed himself for not being with Henry on the *Pennsylvania* and for not being able to save him.

THE CIVIL WAR BREAKS OUT

In the spring of 1859, Clemens received his riverboat pilot's license. Soon, he was earning the princely sum of $250 a month. Clemens loved having money in his pocket even more than he loved the prestige of being a pilot. For the first time in his life, he was able to indulge in fine clothing and expensive meals.

After just two years, his piloting career came to an abrupt end. In April 1861, the first shots were fired in the American Civil War. The war pitted states in the South against states in the North. In part to preserve the institution of slavery, the Southern states wanted to break away and establish a new country, the Confederate States of America. The Northern states wanted to keep the union intact in any way they could, even if it meant Americans battling against Americans. Northern, or Union, troops rushed to blockade the Mississippi, which in effect shut down all riverboat traffic on the river. Some of Clemens's fellow pilots, including Horace Bixby, volunteered for the Union cause. Hailing from a slave state, Clemens had little affection for the North. In fact, with the outbreak of the war, he headed back to Hannibal, largely because he was afraid he would be pressed by the Union into service as a pilot.

At the same time, his allegiance to the Confederacy was far from strong. With a group of old Hannibal friends, he did agree to join the Marion Rangers, a militia group with sympathies for the South. The Rangers, however, were hardly model soldiers—they disbanded after just two weeks. During that time, the Rangers spent most of their days hiding in the woods. At the flimsiest rumor of Union soldiers being near, they ran away, terrified of actually encountering the enemy.

Some of Clemens's Ranger pals later enlisted in the Confederate army. Clemens opted instead to keep on running. His brother Orion, a Union supporter, had worked on the campaign of President Abraham Lincoln. As a reward for his efforts, Orion Clemens was named secretary for the newly formed territory of Nevada by the Lincoln administration. (In the nineteenth century, a region being designated as a territory was an interim step toward it becoming a state.) Sam begged his brother to take him with him. He wanted to get away from everything to do with the Civil War. He also welcomed a chance to start over in the West, an area that then attracted many young men looking to make a name for themselves.

GOING TO THE WILD WEST

After a rollicking three-week stagecoach trip, the brothers arrived in Carson City, Nevada's territorial capital. Clemens worked as a clerk for the territory's legislature, but the job proved too tame for him. He and a friend decided to start a lumber business, but because of Clemens's failure to adequately mind a campfire, the forest they claimed burned to the ground. Clemens then tried his hand at prospecting. Bankrolled by Orion, he set out hoping to find nuggets of silver lying on the ground, just ripe for the picking. After months of hard labor with nothing to show for it, Clemens gave up. But he had not abandoned his dreams of wealth. He wrote to Orion, "I shall never look upon Ma's face again until I am a rich man."[3]

Clemens headed off for Virginia City, Nevada. The frontier town was booming. Nearby, at the Comstock Lode, enormous silver deposits had been discovered. Virginia City was also home to the *Territorial Enterprise*, the first newspaper in Nevada. During his stint as a miner, Clemens had contributed several stories to the paper. They were popular enough to convince the editor to hire Clemens as a reporter.

Although Clemens earned a paltry $25 a week—a dramatic comedown from his high-flying days as a riverboat pilot—he enjoyed his job and the freewheeling atmosphere of the town. Undoubtedly his religious mother would have been stunned to hear that her son spent days and nights in its saloons, theaters, and brothels, chatting with locals and drinking and playing cards with other reporters.

Among his new friends was Charles Farrar Browne. Writing under the pseudonym, or pen name, Artemus Ward, he was then the most popular humorist in the United States. During a three-week visit to Virginia City, Ward got to know Clemens and came away very impressed by the man and his work.

While writing for the *Enterprise*, Clemens used a variety of pseudonyms, from the plain Josh to the fanciful Thomas Jefferson Snodgrass. On February 3, 1863, for a political report from Carson City, he trotted out a new one—Mark

Did you know...

Mark Twain's first readers instantly recognized his pen name as a joke. At the time, "Mark Twain" was a phrase used in riverboat piloting. Boat crews dropped knotted lines of rope into the river to measure the depth of the water. They yelled out "mark twain" when the water was two fathoms, or 12 feet, deep. That depth meant the river was safe to travel.

"Mark Twain" was also possibly a private joke among Clemens and his friends. Supposedly, he had taken to ordering drinks in saloons using the phrase. "Twain" meant he wanted two drinks. "Mark" was an instruction for the barkeep to mark it on his tab, because Clemens did not have the cash on hand to pay him. Whatever its origins, the name Mark Twain stuck. Even some of Clemens's closest associates took to calling him Mark instead of Sam.

Twain. It would become one of the most famous pen names in the history of literature.

A NEW LIFE IN SAN FRANCISCO

In May 1864, the newly minted Mark Twain ran into trouble with another newsman. Afraid his rival was going to challenge him to a duel, Twain decided to get out of town. This time, he headed even farther west, to the bustling city of San Francisco, California. He took a job as a reporter for the *Morning Call*, while also writing pieces for a magazine called the *Golden Era*. Soon Twain was an important member of the San Francisco literary scene, which included famous authors such as Ambrose Bierce and Bret Harte.

The good times did not last long. Twain wrote a story that condemned the brutal treatment of Chinese workers at the hands of the San Francisco police. When his editor refused to run it, Twain sent it to his old paper in Virginia City. The move angered his editor enough to fire Twain. He was devastated. Unemployed for months, Twain avoided his friends, feeling too ashamed to face them. He even contemplated suicide.

At a loss over what to do next, Twain finally headed out to Angels Camp, a mining camp in the foothills of the Sierra Mountains. As the winter rains set in, his latest effort to strike it rich proved to be a dud. But while there, he heard from the miners a tall tale about a frog-jumping contest. In the end, that story would bring him far more wealth than any gold nugget ever could have. Twain wrote it down, adding his own touches and flourishes, and sent it to Artemus Ward. Ward loved it and submitted it to the *New York Saturday Press* for publication. The East Coast press acclaimed the story "Jim Smiley and His Jumping Frog," which was soon reprinted in papers all over the country, introducing Americans everywhere to a funny young writer named Mark Twain.

Twain went back to San Francisco. He did not return with a bag of gold as he had hoped, but with something more valuable—a new determination to establish himself as a humorist. In the fall of 1865, he wrote to Orion, telling him, "I *have* had a 'call' to literature, of a low order—i.e. humorous. It is nothing to be proud of, but it is my strongest suit."[4]

The following year, Twain was hired by two California papers to take a trip to the Sandwich Islands (now Hawaii) and write a series of travel letters describing what he saw there. His earlier efforts to write amusing letters to his family about his travels in the East proved to be excellent training for the assignment. During his four-month adventure, he provided his editors with clever letters about visiting a sugar plantation, hiking through a volcano crater, and meeting King Kamehameha V at his royal palace.

"THE TROUBLE TO BEGIN AT 8"

Twain's letters were wildly popular in California. A friend suggested he capitalize on their success by transforming them into a humor piece he could deliver on the lecture circuit. In a world without television and movies, people often enjoyed a night out at a theater to listen to speakers offering interesting and entertaining lectures.

Twain was completely horrified by the idea. What if no one showed up? Or even worse, what if no one laughed? In addition, he worried about the expense of the enterprise. He would have to rent a hall and pay to advertise the lecture.

Lacking enough savings, Twain would have to borrow the $200 needed to stage a lecture, without much confidence that he would be able to earn it back.

Despite his trepidation, Twain decided to give the lecture circuit a try. He rented San Francisco's Academy of Music and took out advertisements for his lecture, titled "Our Fellow Savages of the Sandwich Isles." The ads informed would-be ticket buyers, "Doors open at 7 o'clock. The Trouble to begin at 8."[5]

On the day of the show, October 2, 1866, Twain arrived at the Academy of Music agitated and weak. Far too nervous to eat and sure he had made a terrible mistake, he headed backstage. His fears that no one would come to his talk were soon eased. Waiting alone, he listened as more and more people entered the hall. As the starting time neared, he heard impatient audience members, eager to hear Mark Twain speak, begin to cheer and stamp their feet.

Finally, it was eight o'clock. Twain walked onstage. Despite the glare of the lights, he could see the house was packed, full of prominent Californians. Even the state's governor was there. As Twain later recalled:

> The tumult in my heart and brain and legs continued a full minute before I could gain any command over myself. Then I recognized the charity and the friendliness in the faces before me, and little by little my fright melted away, and I began to talk.[6]

Twain talked and talked, in an exaggerated Western drawl, for a full hour. And the audience responded with titters, giggles, and full belly laughs in just the right places. The evening was a great success for Twain, critically and financially. He received rave reviews. But just as important, in only one night, he had netted $400. Suddenly, Samuel Clemens had discovered the way to become the rich man he had always wanted to be. All he had to do was transform himself into a character named Mark Twain.

A circa 1920s photo of the family home of Olivia Langdon, who became Mark Twain's wife. Langdon met Samuel Clemens through her brother Charles in December 1867.

4

Success at Last

MARK TWAIN'S SUCCESSFUL lecture was no one-time fluke. Over the next month, he delivered the same talk in mining towns throughout California and Nevada with the same results. Audiences cheered him wherever he performed.

While the acclaim was pleasing to Twain, he wanted more. He still hankered for the approval of Easterners, specifically New Yorkers. As he once wrote, "Make your mark in New York, and you are a made man. With a New York endorsement you may travel the country over, without fear—but without it you are speculating on a dangerous issue."[1] When in late 1866 the newspaper *Alta California* gave him an assignment to write

50 travel letters, Twain happily left the West and headed to New York, determined this time to win over the city.

Day and night, Twain was out and about, discovering everything the city had to offer. He went to plays, museums, the opera—any place that might provide an amusing anecdote for his California readers. But soon city life began to wear on him. In San Francisco, he was a big deal in the literary scene. In New York, he was just another aspiring

Did you know...

For the amusement of Eastern readers, Mark Twain described his adventures in the West in *Roughing It* (1872). Decades later, this travel book inspired the creation of one of the most famous American cartoon characters—Wile E. Coyote from the Road Runner cartoons. Chuck Jones, the creator of Wile E. Coyote, read Twain's book when he was seven years old. He never forgot Twain's description of the coyotes he saw: "The coyote is a long, slim, sick and sorry-looking skeleton, with a gray wolf-skin stretched over it, a tolerably bushy tail that forever sags down with a despairing expression of forsakenness and misery. . . . The coyote is a living, breathing allegory of Want."* Charmed by Twain's portrait of this sad, scrawny animal always desperate for a meal, Jones made dozens of cartoons starring his own famous coyote.

*Shelley Fisher Fishkin, *Lighting Out for the Territory: Reflections on Mark Twain and American Culture.* New York: Oxford University Press, 1996, p. 149.

writer among many. Twain was still able to fill houses when he lectured, but, out of fear no one would show up, he gave away so many tickets that he lost money on each performance. In the spring of 1867, he saw the publication of his first book, *The Celebrated Jumping Frog of Calaveras County, and Other Sketches*, but that too proved disappointing. The book sold badly and convinced Twain he was destined to be a failure as a writer. In a letter home, he wrote, "I am so worthless that it seems to me I never do anything or accomplish anything that lingers in my mind as a pleasant memory."[2]

A TOUR OF THE OLD WORLD

Fed up with New York, Twain accepted an assignment in June 1867 that would take him far from the city. The *Alta California* and two New York papers agreed to pay his passage on the *Quaker City*, a steamship bound for a tour of Europe and the Middle East. Twain was to send back letters about his travels for publication. The cruise was the first of its kind. The idea of a pleasure trip to the Old World was then new, although over the next few decades, such tours would become increasingly popular among prosperous Americans.

Twain was one of about 70 passengers. Most were sober and somber Midwesterners who he found rather boring. He tried to fit in by joining in shuffleboard games, public readings, debates, and prayer services. But Twain much preferred the company of a few select men he became friendly with. Calling themselves the Nighthawks, they stayed up drinking, smoking, and playing cards long after their more serious-minded fellow travelers had gone to bed.

Twain also struck up a friendship with one of the female passengers, Mary Fairbanks. The wife of a wealthy publisher from Cleveland, Ohio, she took a liking to Twain but could see that the young man from Hannibal was still a bit rough around the edges. With Twain's encouragement, Fairbanks tutored him in the habits and mores of polite society. She also read his travel letters and offered suggestions. From Fairbanks, Twain learned what type of language and stories might offend the more refined members of the Eastern elite whom he was so desperate to impress.

AN OFFER FROM A PUBLISHER

Despite Fairbanks's lessons, Twain did manage to upset some of the other passengers with his depictions of them in his letters. Their displeasure became a minor news story after the *Quaker City* returned to New York. The story caught the attention of Elisha Bliss, head of the American Publishing Company in Hartford, Connecticut. Where others saw a controversy, he saw a great publicity hook. He contacted Twain and asked if he would be interested in expanding his travel letters into a book.

The American Publishing Company was a subscription publisher. More high-toned publishing houses sold their books through bookstores. Subscription publishers, however, marketed their books through traveling salesmen, who went to small towns and rural communities where there were no bookstores. Going from house to house, they showed potential customers sales materials and tried to convince them to sign up for a copy of the proposed book once it was published.

Families might buy only two or three subscription books a year, so subscription publishers had to make sure they were offering products that gave their customers their money's worth. The books had to be fairly long and include hundreds of illustrations. Travel books tended to be big sellers, but Bliss was taking a risk in marketing a book by Twain. No one had tried selling by subscription a book of humorous travel sketches like the one he wanted Twain to write.

Twain was not sure about the project. He wrote to Bliss asking how much money he could realistically expect to see from the book. As he explained, the matter had "a degree of importance for me which is almost beyond my own comprehension."[3] When Bliss assured him that both of them could stand to see a healthy payday, Twain signed on. In the next few months, he wrote furiously, adding more and more stories in order to deliver a book of the needed heft.

COURTING LIVY LANGDON

Just as he began working on the book, Twain was invited to a party in New York by Charley Langdon, one of the Night-hawks whom Twain cavorted with aboard the *Quaker City*. Twain surely wanted to see his friend, but he had another reason to attend. On the ship, Langdon had shown Twain a miniature painting of his sister Olivia, who went by the nickname Livy. Twain was instantly smitten. The party gave him a chance to see Livy in person.

At the party, Twain was charmed enough to jump at the chance to visit Charley at the Langdon family home the following summer. The Langdons were the wealthiest family in Elmira, New York. Twain, while impressed by their grand three-story house, was even more taken by the pretty Livy. She was well educated, devoutly religious, and physically fragile. The rough and worldly Twain hardly seemed a proper match for Livy, but he did not care. Within a few days, he asked her to marry him. She refused but told him he could write to her as long as he addressed his letters to Charley so her parents would not know they were corresponding. He wrote her more than 180 letters over the next year and a half. Each one, she numbered and carefully preserved.

As he traveled on a lecture tour, speaking about his foreign adventures, Livy wrote him letters imploring him to become the type of man she ought to marry. She urged him to read the Bible. She begged him to stop drinking, smoking, and swearing. She also pored over the pages of his book, suggesting changes to make it more appealing to people in her social circle. Twain was delighted by her letters and declared he could become a Christian gentleman if that was the way to win her love. Although he failed to make good on his promises to give up alcohol and tobacco, in the end Livy could not resist him. During Twain's Thanksgiving visit to her family in 1868, she agreed to be his wife.

MAKING HIS CASE

Livy's parents were stunned by the engagement. Her father, Jervis Langdon, in particular, was not so sure about Twain. He told the couple to keep their plans a secret until he could in good conscience give them his blessing. With Twain's permission, Jervis performed a background check on his potential son-in-law by asking Twain's friends in the West to attest to his character. Their responses hardly helped the young man's case. According to Twain, "They said with one accord that I got drunk oftener than was necessary & that I was wild and Godless, idle, lecherous & a discontented & an unsettled rover & they could not recommend any girl of high character & social position to marry me."[4] The reports were hardly a surprise, because Twain himself had already admitted to his past sins. Impressed by Twain's honesty and his passion for Livy, Langdon blessed the marriage.

He was, however, still concerned about Twain's lifestyle. Langdon insisted he settle down. Twain bought part ownership in the *Buffalo Express*, a newspaper in Buffalo, New York, using a sizable loan from Langdon. After their marriage on February 2, 1870, Twain and his bride received an equally generous wedding gift from Langdon: When they arrived in Buffalo, they discovered Livy's father had bought them a grand house, completely furnished and staffed by three servants. Still thinking of himself as a poor boy from Hannibal, Twain could barely believe the life he was living. In a letter to his in-laws, he jokingly called himself "Little Sammy in Fairyland."[5]

The early months of his marriage also seemed almost too wonderful to be real. Having grown up in a tense and emotionally cold household, Twain had been surprised by the Langdon family's open affection for one another. He was thrilled to have Livy introduce him to a similarly rich emotional life. Her warmth encouraged him to talk with her honestly and, at her urging, to recall painful memories of his youth that he had tried unsuccessfully to suppress. It was a revelation to Twain that he could be this close to another person. As Twain once recalled, "I was born *reserved* as to endearments of speech, and caresses, and hers broke upon me as the summer waves break on Gibraltar."[6]

THE INNOCENTS ABROAD

In addition to living in a beautiful home with a wife he adored, Twain was reeling from his greatest professional success to date. In June 1869, his book about his tour overseas, *The Innocents Abroad, or The New Pilgrims' Progress*, was published. It was an instant hit and sold 70,000 copies in just its first year in print. Almost giddily, Twain wrote to an old friend, "We keep six steam presses and a paper mill going *night and day*, and still we can't catch up on the orders."[7] In Twain's lifetime, *The Innocents Abroad* was the best selling of all his works.

The book was a twist on the travel books readers were accustomed to. Most were written with great authority and tended to praise the beauties and wonders of the Old World, which most Americans could never expect to see themselves. Twain's first-person narrator, in contrast, did not seem to know much about anything. Portraying himself as a western bumpkin, he created a comical character that readers embraced. The pose, however, also allowed him to question the assumptions of most travel writers. In the book, Twain continually describes Europe not as glorious and sophisticated, but as shabby and rundown. He continually laughs at the idea that travelers are supposed to be in awe of artworks created by people from long ago. The Twain character infuriates his guides by asking, "Is he dead?" whenever they speak of European artists in hushed and reverent tones.

In this way, the book addressed Americans' anxiety about their own culture. The United States had not yet reached its one-hundredth birthday. As citizens of such a young country, many Americans often felt culturally inferior to Europeans. By making his narrator so inexperienced that he did not know how superior European culture supposedly was, Twain was able to slyly call that superiority into question. He suggested that the ignorant Mark Twain character might not be so stupid after all. Maybe he was the only one not influenced by old assumptions, the only one who could look at things with a clear eye. Near the end of the book, the narrator declares, "I can see easily enough that if I wish to profit by this tour and come to a correct understanding of the matters of interest connected with it, I must studiously and faithfully unlearn a great many things I have somehow absorbed."[8]

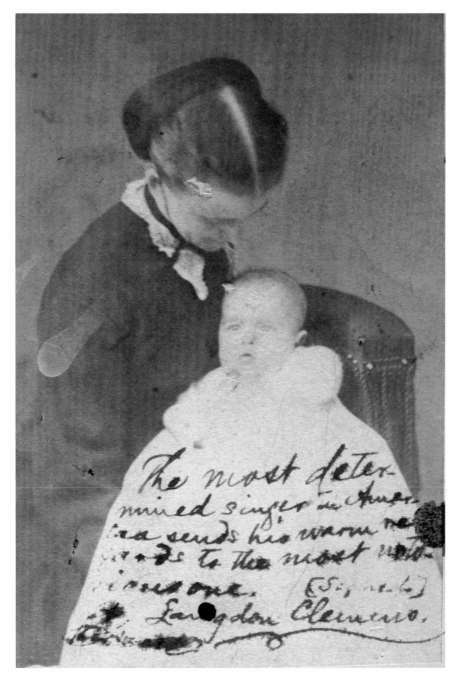

A photograph of Mark Twain's only son, Langdon, held in his aunt's arms. The author inscribed the photo to his friend Bret Harte, an American author and poet, best remembered for writing about the pioneering life in California.

In this way, the book flattered its American readers. If European culture were not in fact superior, it implied, then American culture might not really be so inferior. If Europe could be seen as old and dingy, a relict of the past, then the United States could be seen as new and exciting, the promise of the future.

The Innocents Abroad was not just a popular success. It was also a triumph with critics. William Dean Howells, the associate editor of the *Atlantic Monthly*—then the most influential literary magazine in the United States—was particularly impressed by Twain's sophomore book. He wrote:

> Under his *nom de plume* of Mark Twain, Mr. Clemens is well known to the very large world of newspaper-readers; and this book ought to secure him better than the uncertain standing of a popular favorite. It is no business of ours to fix his rank among the humorists California has given us, but we think he is, in an entirely different way from all the others, quite worthy of the company of the best.[9]

MOVING TO HARTFORD

To Twain, it seemed as though life could not get any better. He was right. Just six months after their wedding, Livy was dealt a cruel blow. In August 1870, her father suddenly died. Now pregnant, the ever-frail Livy fell apart. A close friend moved in to help care for her, but the woman soon contracted typhoid fever and died in the Twains' bed. In November, Livy gave birth to a son, whom she named Langdon to honor her father. Arriving two months premature, Langdon was a constant worry to his parents, who feared he would not survive infancy.

As was his habit, Twain decided the solution to their problems was to move. He sold off their house and his interest in the *Buffalo Express* and relocated the family to

The Mark Twain House in Hartford, Connecticut, where the author and his family lived from 1874 to 1891. The 19-room mansion is notable for the major works Twain wrote while he lived there, including The Gilded Age, The Adventures of Tom Sawyer, The Prince and the Pauper, Life on the Mississippi, Adventures of Huckleberry Finn, A Tramp Abroad, *and* A Connecticut Yankee in King Arthur's Court.

Hartford, Connecticut. He had visited the city when writing travel letters for the *Alta California* three years earlier. Of Hartford, he wrote, "Of all the beautiful towns it has been my fortune to see this is the chief. . . . You do not know what beauty is if you have not been here."[10] The Twains settled down in Nook Farm, Hartford's wealthiest neighborhood. In this idyllic setting, with its stately mansions and colorful gardens, Twain would begin the happiest and most productive years of his life.

Mark Twain seated with his family outside their home in Hartford, Connecticut. From left, his daughter, Clara; his wife, Olivia; his daughter, Jean; Twain; and his daughter, Susy. The family dog's name is Hash.

America's Writer

MOVING THE FAMILY to Hartford was expensive. To pay his bills, Twain went back on the lecture circuit. He wrote Livy every day from whatever hotel in whatever town he found himself. But his letters did little to soothe Livy's dismay at their separation. "I *can not* and I WILL NOT think about your being away from me this way every year,"[1] she announced in one of her letters.

Adding to her anxiety, Livy was pregnant again. In March 1872, she gave birth to a daughter named Olivia Susan, whom the family called Susy. To her parents' relief, she was as hardy as Langdon was sickly. About two months later, Twain took the ailing boy on a carriage ride. Langdon soon developed diphtheria and died. Just as he had after Henry's death, the grieving Twain came up with a convoluted way to blame himself. He was sure Langdon would never have died if he had not taken him outside on that cold spring day.

ROUGHING IT AND *THE GILDED AGE*

Just before Langdon's death, Twain's follow-up to *The Innocents Abroad* was published. Originally called *The Innocents at Home*, the book was retitled *Roughing It*. Like his first best seller, *Roughing It* was a travel book. Instead of documenting Twain's experiences in the Old World, it recounted his adventures in the West during the Civil War era. He represented himself as the same type of naïve character as he did in *The Innocents Abroad*. Much of the book dealt with his failure at every job he took on, from lumberman to prospector to writer. The book parodied the popular nineteenth-century idea of the West as the great land of opportunity where any ambitious young man could make it.

Roughing It was another popular success for Twain. It also received much critical praise, particularly from Charles Dudley Warner, the editor of the *Hartford Courant*: "[W]e are inclined to think that, on the whole, it contains the best picture of frontier mining life that has been written. . . . It would be unpleasant to read about it, if the author did not constantly relieve the dreadful picture with strokes of humor."[2] Warner was not only a champion of Twain's writing but also a personal friend and neighbor. Soon after arriving in Hartford, Twain had been embraced by its elite society. He was invited to join the Monday Evening Club, a group of prominent literary figures, businessmen, and politicians that regularly met for dinner and conversation. Twain also became friendly with another neighbor, Harriet

Beecher Stowe. Because of her antislavery novel *Uncle Tom's Cabin* (1852), she was then one of the most famous authors in the United States.

Twain's next project had its origins in his Hartford social circle. One night in January 1873, Twain and Livy were having dinner with Warner and his wife. The men began making merciless fun of the women's taste in novels. Their wives shot back by challenging them to do better. Then and there, Twain and Warner decided to collaborate on their own novel. The result was *The Gilded Age: A Tale of Today* (1873). The book lampooned American society in the 1870s. Much of its satire was aimed at the era's political corruption and wild financial speculation. The title has since become the name used to describe the post–Civil War boom period that, because of the rapid growth of industry, saw the concentration of incredible wealth in the hands of a select group of industrialists and financiers.

Aside from its title, the biggest legacy of *The Gilded Age* was its central character, Captain Eschol Sellers. Sellers is an eternal optimist, convinced that every business idea he has is going to make him a fortune. Sellers's repeated assertion, "There's millions in it," became a catchphrase in Twain's day. Twain modeled the character after a cousin, but he also admitted that there was a bit of Sellers in himself as well.

THE TWAIN FAMILY HOME

Throughout his life, Twain was obsessed with money— both making it and spending it. His most extravagant expense of all was the house he had built for his family in Hartford. When Twain arrived in the city, he bought a five-acre plot adjoining Harriet Beecher Stowe's property. He then hired architect Edward Tuckerman Potter to

Mark Twain looking out of the window of his study at his in-laws residence at Quarry Farm in Elmira, New York. In 1874, Susan and Theodore Crane surprised their brother-in-law with this study, which was located about 100 yards (91 meters) from the main house overlooking the Chemung River Valley.

design the eccentric mansion, which the *Hartford Daily Times* described as "one of the oddest looking buildings in the State ever designed for a dwelling, if not in the whole country."[3] With construction beginning in 1874, the three-story house would eventually have 19 rooms. Its numerous bay windows and balconies offered spectacular views of the town Twain loved.

Originally, a large room on the first floor was supposed to be his study. But with the addition of two more daughters to the family—Clara in 1874 and Jean in 1880—Twain surrendered his study to his three girls for use as a playroom and a classroom. He moved his desk and his billiards table to a room on the top floor. When he was not working, he asked friends over for a drink or a game of pool in this sanctuary.

When work on the house began, Livy's sister Susan invited Twain's family to spend the summer at Quarry Farm, her home in Elmira, New York. The visit would become an annual event for some 20 summers. To give Twain a place to work without interruption from the girls and their cousins, Susan had a private study built especially

Did you know...

When Susy Clemens was 13 years old, she decided to write the story of her famous father's life. Working in secret, she completed a biography of Twain. Her mother found the manuscript and shared it with her husband. Twain was touched by Susy's project and said it was the greatest compliment he had ever received in his life. Portions of Susy's biography appear in the 2010 children's book *The Extraordinary Mark Twain (According to Susy)*.

for him on a hilltop overlooking a shimmering river, green farmland, and lush forests. Twain once called it "the quietest of all quiet places."[4]

WRITING *TOM SAWYER*

During his second summer at Quarry Farm, Twain finished a new novel, *The Adventures of Tom Sawyer*. For the book, Twain called up the childhood memories that his conversations with Livy had helped refresh. The story took place before the Civil War in the Mississippi River town of St. Petersburg, a fictional version of Hannibal, Missouri. The title character was an imaginative, mischievous 12-year-old boy, largely based on Twain's vision of himself as a child. The novel traces Tom's efforts to win the heart of a pretty classmate, Becky Thatcher, and Tom's various adventures with his friend Huckleberry Finn, the son of the town drunk.

Although St. Petersburg and Hannibal bore some resemblance, Twain painted a portrait of his childhood home that was far more idyllic than it actually was. Now in his forties, Twain returned to the world of his youth with nostalgia, presenting it as a simpler place and time. This longing for an earlier and simpler era struck a chord with Twain's contemporaries. Following the Civil War, the United States went through a wrenching economic and social transformation, as large numbers of Americans moved from farms to factories and from rural settings to urban centers. Dizzied by rapid change, readers were comforted by looking backward to a time when, at least in their imaginations, everything in life seemed easier.

Twain was contemptuous of children's literature, which in the nineteenth century more often focused on teaching children moral lessons than offering them a good story.

Reflecting this bias, he insisted to his friend and supporter William Dean Howells that *Tom Sawyer* was not a book for children: "It is *not* a boy's book, at all. It will only be read by adults. It was only written for adults."[5] Both Howells and Livy, however, suggested that he was missing its potential to delight young readers. At their urging, he edited out profanity and some disturbing images to make it more acceptable for children. Even so, his publisher marketed it as a book for adults, as Twain wanted. To Twain's disappointment, *Tom Sawyer* did not sell well initially, although it has since become one of his most read books worldwide.

HUCK'S VOICE

Before *Tom Sawyer* was even published, Twain started working on a sequel. In writing the novel, he had become intrigued by the character of Huck Finn. Twain thought Tom Sawyer's friend deserved a book of his own. But as he began writing, *Adventures of Huckleberry Finn* quickly began to shape into a very different book than *Tom Sawyer*. For one thing, *Tom Sawyer* was written in the third person. The technique gave the reader some distance from the children in the story, just as Twain had felt in remembering his youth from an adult perspective. In *Huckleberry Finn*, however, Twain decided to let the title character tell his own story. Because Huck is an uneducated boy from a frontier town, the book had to be told in vernacular—that is, the narrative had to use only the words and speech patterns a boy like Huck would use.

Twain had written in vernacular before, mostly notably in "A True Story, Repeated Word for Word as I Heard It." The story, published in the *Atlantic Monthly*, was drawn from a conversation Twain had with Mary Ann Cord, the

African-American cook at Quarry Farm. In summer afternoons, she would join Livy, Livy's sister, and the three girls on the porch, while Twain read the pages he had written that day. Struck by Cord's pleasant demeanor, he once asked her how she had lived to be 60 without ever having any trouble in her life. Cord corrected him. She recounted her years as a slave and the breakup of her family by her owner, making it clear that she had seen plenty of trouble. Using Mary Ann's strong slave dialect, Twain wrote down her words. The story was unique at the time. Slave dialect had been used in literature to ridicule blacks, but never to ennoble their struggles.

Writing an entire book in Huck's voice would be similarly daring. It was then thought by literary tastemakers that reading books should be an elevating experience and therefore they should be written using proper English, with respect to the rules of spelling, usage, and grammar. A book with an unschooled narrator, written in slang and other nonstandard language, would surely strike many critics as impossibly vulgar.

A BURST OF CREATIVITY

After writing the first quarter of *Huckleberry Finn* in 1876, Twain was stymied. Unable to figure out where the story was going, he put the manuscript aside. He wrote to Howells about the aborted project: "I like it only tolerably well, as far as I have got, and may possibly pigeonhole it or burn the manuscript when it is done."[6]

Twain then turned his attention to other projects, returning to *Huckleberry Finn* from time to time with little success. In 1880, he published *A Tramp Abroad*, another travel book. It was the product of a 17-month trip the family took to Europe, largely to save money. Living at the Hartford

Huckleberry Finn, played by Eddie Hodges, and Jim, played by Archie Moore, crouch down in a publicity shot for the 1960 film, The Adventures of Huckleberry Finn, directed by Michael Curtiz. The growing friendship between Huck and Jim is the main focus of Twain's masterpiece.

house had grown insanely expensive, with the numerous servants and tutors Twain insisted they hire. In 1882, he published *The Prince and the Pauper*. Set in sixteenth-century England, the novel told the story of two boys, a prince and an impoverished child, who switch identities. The plot allowed Twain to examine the disparities in the lives of the rich and the poor. Hailing its refined use of language, Livy declared it his greatest book.

His next major work was inspired by a conversation with Reverend Joseph Twichell, who had become his best friend in Hartford. The two men liked to take long walks together. One day, during their meandering conversation, Twain started to reminisce about his days as a riverboat pilot. Twichell excitedly told him that was an excellent subject for an article. Never having thought of writing about his days on the Mississippi, Twain wrote to Howells, asking what he thought of the idea. Howells was as enthusiastic as Twichell, and Twain wrote a series of articles for the *Atlantic Monthly*. Deciding to turn them into a full-length book, eventually published as *Life on the Mississippi* (1883), Twain took a trip to Missouri in the spring of 1882 to see that world again. The visit was sobering. Railroads had replaced riverboats as the primary means of transporting goods. As a result, many of the once-thriving towns along the river were experiencing hard times. The trip also reminded him of the profound impact slavery had had on the world in which he grew up.

Twain's trip to the Mississippi reawakened his interest in *Huckleberry Finn*. In the summer of 1883, he went back to the book and was suddenly writing furiously. The manuscript he produced was much darker than *Tom Sawyer*. In the earlier book, Twain barely mentioned slavery. In *Huckleberry Finn*, the subject took center stage through the relationship between Huck and the slave Jim. After running away from his abusive alcoholic father, Huck travels the Mississippi on a raft with Jim, who is trying to escape into freedom. Like the young Samuel Clemens, Huck at first regards blacks as inferior to whites. But as he comes to respect and even love Jim, he has to reexamine everything he has been told about slavery.

His internal conflict comes to a head when he decides to write Jim's owner to tell her where Jim is. Huck has been taught in his church that helping Jim escape is a sin that would surely send him to Hell. After writing the letter, Huck is initially relieved: He has saved his soul by doing the right thing. But then he remembers his fond feelings toward Jim. After speaking the novel's most famous line— "All right, then, I'll *go* to hell"[7]—Huck tears up the letter.

SELLING *HUCKLEBERRY FINN*

Feeling his own publisher was not doing enough to market his books, Mark Twain decided to publish them himself. In 1884, he started a publishing firm called Webster & Company. As the name indicated, the company was supposedly run by his nephew by marriage, Charles L. Webster, who had been helping Twain manage his business affairs. Twain, however, was the driving force behind it.

The first book to be published by Webster & Company was *Adventures of Huckleberry Finn.* Determined to make it a success, Twain went on a lecture tour, largely to promote the book. During his lectures, Twain included excerpts from the novel to excite the reading public's interest in it. The most popular was the ending, which, according to a reporter for the *Cincinnati Enquirer*, "created roars of laughter"[8] in the lecture hall. Twain himself wrote in a letter to Livy, "[I]t's the biggest card I've got in my whole repetoire."[9]

At the end of *Huckleberry Finn*, Tom Sawyer makes a guest appearance. By that point in the novel, Jim has already been captured. Although both Tom and Huck find out that Jim's owner has died and freed him in her will, they do not tell Jim. Tom instead invents an elaborate ruse to "free" the already free Jim, and Huck plays along. To modern readers, the game seems remarkably cruel to Jim. But in Twain's day, according to the *Indianapolis Journal*, audiences were "tickled to death with the story of Huck Finn and Tom Sawyer in their arrangement of 'Jim's' escape from the cabin."[10]

In his company's publicity material, Twain played up the role of Tom Sawyer in the book. The subtitle listed in all the sales literature was "Tom Sawyer's Comrade." The illustrator, handpicked by Twain, was E.W. Kemble, who had made a career of creating stereotyped images of blacks that had their origins in minstrel shows—a popular form of entertainment in which white performers with their faces blackened depicted African-Americans as comic buffoons. Although Twain allowed Huck to recognize Jim as fully human, through the book's ending and art, he also diluted any guilt his white readers might feel about slavery by making Jim the target of ridicule.

"WHATEVER I TOUCH TURNS TO GOLD"

When *Huckleberry Finn* was published in 1885, Twain was worried about how it would be received. He was not, however, concerned as much about his depiction of slavery as he was about the vernacular language used by Huck. In fact, some reviewers and readers did take offense at what they considered the novel's coarse language. Among them was the writer Louisa May Alcott, author of the famous children's novel *Little Women* (1868). She wrote:

> If Mr. Clemens cannot think of something better to tell our pure-minded lads and lasses, he had best stop writing for them. It is time that this influential pseudonym should cease

to carry into homes and libraries unworthy productions. The trouble with Mr. Clemens is that he has no reliable sense of propriety.[11]

The public library in Concord, Massachusetts, banned the book, calling it "trash and suitable only for the slums."[12] Twain the author was annoyed, but Twain the publisher was delighted. "That will sell 25,000 copies for us sure,"[13] he declared.

Webster & Company's next book was the memoirs of former president and Civil War hero Ulysses S. Grant. Learning Grant was bankrupt, Twain paid him a huge sum for the manuscript in 1884. Just days after making his final corrections to the book, Grant died of cancer. With the publicity surrounding Grant's death, sales of the book skyrocketed.

In 1885, when Mark Twain turned 50, he could look back on a half century of life with some satisfaction. He had a beautiful home and a loving family. He had just experienced an astoundingly prolific period, in which he had produced some of the greatest works of his career. He had also started a publishing company that was already extremely success-ful. Twain's good fortune was almost overwhelming. At the time, Twain wrote, "I am frightened at the proportions of my prosperity. It seems to me that whatever I touch turns to gold."[14] Fate would prove that Twain indeed had reason to be afraid. From the mighty heights he had climbed, the upcoming fall would be long and far.

The Billiard Room in the Mark Twain House in Hartford, Connecticut. In addition to entertaining friends here, Twain used this private domain to write some of his greatest works.

6

Debt and Disaster

AFTER THE PUBLICATION of *Adventures of Huckleberry Finn*, Mark Twain wanted to make a drastic change in his life. He was tired of lecturing and of worrying about how the public and the critics would receive his work. Twain began thinking of new ways to make money so he would be free to live and write as he liked.

It was a challenge, considering how much Twain spent to maintain his Hartford home. In addition to his staff of servants, Twain constantly poured cash into renovating the grand house. He even hired Louis Comfort Tiffany, one of the most famous designers in the country, to create intricate stained-glass windows for the first floor. To Twain, the house was a symbol of his success, so he was willing to do anything to make it more impressive to visitors. He often hosted lavish dinners for famous guests, including actor Edwin Booth, adventurer Henry M. Stanley, and former general William Tecumseh Sherman. Altogether, Twain's yearly household expenses grew to about $30,000, the equivalent of about $230,000 in today's currency.

INVESTING IN THE FUTURE

One of Twain's moneymaking schemes involved expanding his publishing company. The success of *Huckleberry Finn* and of the memoirs of Ulysses S. Grant convinced him that Webster & Company was a veritable goldmine. Following the model of the Grant book, Twain began signing up other famous people to write their life stories. His roster of authors included Civil War leaders General George McClellan and General Philip Sheridan, as well as Elizabeth Custer, widow of Lieutenant General George Armstrong Custer, who was famous for his role in the U.S. military's wars against American Indians of the Great Plains. Twain had the highest hopes for an official biography of Pope Leo XIII, which he was sure every Catholic in the world would want to buy.

Twain also began to invest in a series of new inventions. At the time, growing industrialization and new technologies had made the mass production of many new exciting products possible. Twain was personally thrilled by these inventions, such as the telephone and the typewriter. He became the first person in Hartford to install a telephone in his house and was one of the first authors to submit a typewritten manuscript to a publisher.

Although Twain saw promise in a number of new inventions, including a telegraph system, an engraving process, and a steam generator, he was convinced the machine that would make him rich was a typesetter built by Hartford inventor James W. Paige. From his days of working in print shops as a young man, Twain knew exactly how difficult setting type by hand could be. A mechanized typesetter, he imagined, could do the work of half a dozen men. Every newspaper would jump at the chance to buy one. Twain wrote to his brother, telling him that all the new gadgets coming out would pale in comparison to Paige's machine, once the design was finalized: "Telephones, telegraphs, locomotives, cotton-gins, sewing machines, Babbage calculators, Jacquard looms, perfecting presses, all mere toys, simplicities! The Paige Compositor marches alone and far in the land of human inventions."[1]

Twain gave Paige $30,000 for half ownership in his typesetter. Paige continued to work on his machine, always promising Twain that, any day now, the design would be perfected. From time to time, he asked Twain for more

Did you know...

Mark Twain not only invested in inventions; he also invented a few himself. Twain held patents for a self-adjusting garter and a memory-building board game, and for his own use he made special notebooks with tear-away tabs to help him keep his place. Just one of his inventions ever made any money: a self-pasting scrapbook.

money, and Twain always obliged him. After all, the paltry thousands he was giving to Paige seemed a tiny sacrifice given the many millions he would stand to make when the typesetter was ready to market.

A CONNECTICUT YANKEE

While waiting for his big payday, Twain began work on a new book. This one, though, he was writing just for fun. He wrote about the project to his friend Mary Fairbanks, explaining that the manuscript "is to be my holiday amusement for six days every summer the rest of my life. Of course I do not expect to publish it; nor indeed any other book."[2]

Twain got the idea for the book, *A Connecticut Yankee in King Arthur's Court* (1889), while he was touring to promote *Huckleberry Finn.* On the tour, he often shared the lectern with New Orleans writer George Washington Cable. Cable gave Twain a copy of *Le Morte D'Arthur* (1485) by Sir Thomas Malory. It told the story of the adventures of King Arthur and his knights in sixth-century England. The two men loved the book and took to talking to each other in its antiquated language, enjoying the confusion of other travelers who overheard them in railroad cars and hotel lobbies.

Twain began wondering what would happen if a nineteenth-century man were transported back to King Arthur's time. He thought the idea was flush with comic potential in the contrast between old ways and modern times. He chose as his hero a factory foreman and inventor named Hank Morgan. Instead of seeing sixth-century England through the romantic lens of *Le Morte D'Arthur*, Morgan was full of disdain for this world. To him, it was a place of filth, squalor, and injustice, where the vast majority

The infamous Paige Compositor, as seen on exhibit at the Mark Twain House in Hartford, Connecticut. The author sunk so much money into this worthless typesetter that he later found himself having to declare bankruptcy.

of peasants were forced to labor for the benefit of a tiny aristocracy. As Morgan explained, "[H]ere I was, in a country where a right to say how the country should be governed was restricted to six persons in each thousand of its population. . . . It seemed to me that what the nine hundred and ninety-four dupes needed was a new deal."[3] These words would inspire President Franklin Delano Roosevelt in the

1930s to give the name "New Deal" to his policies designed to help Americans survive the Great Depression.

MONEY TROUBLES

Although Twain intended *Connecticut Yankee* to be nothing more than a personal project to amuse him, by the summer of 1887 he was struggling to finish it as fast as he could. He desperately needed money. Almost none of the inventions in which he had invested were panning out. Worst of all, the Paige typesetter proved to be a money sink. Paige talked a good game, always promising that the machine would make them both rich, if only Twain exercised a little more patience and invested a little more money. Twain's publishing company was not making the profits he had hoped, but whatever money it did make he began funneling into his other investments. In time, Twain even began borrowing money to keep his dreams for the Paige typesetter alive.

In order to hold up this financial house of cards, Twain rushed through the *Connecticut Yankee* manuscript. His anxiety over his financial troubles and growing doubts about the worth of modern technology seeped into the book's bitter ending. Morgan wants to improve the lives of medieval peasants by introducing them to such technology, but in the end, he introduces them to weapons that lead only to mass slaughter.

The darkness of the book seemed lost on Twain's readers. It was sold as a patriotic book, one that trumpeted American ingenuity and freedom. A reviewer for the *Boston Herald* wrote:

> Throughout the book there is a steady flowing undercurrent
> of earnest purpose, and the pages are eloquent with a true
> American love of freedom, a sympathy with the rights of the

common people, and an indignant hatred of oppression of the poor, the lowly and the weak, by the rich, the powerful and the proud.[4]

In 1891, Twain took his family to Europe. Livy was feeling ill, and her doctors advised that the climate there might aid her recovery. Twain also wanted a break from the financial drain of the Hartford house. In Europe, the family could still live well on far less money.

A PROLIFIC PERIOD

In addition to Twain's failing finances, new emotional strains were beginning to fracture the family. Twain had a difficult personality. When spending time with Livy and his girls, he always expected to be the center of attention. He also was prone to sudden fits of rage that frightened them. When the girls were young, the family remained close, despite these tensions. But as they became young women, they were less indulgent of their father. Twain also refused to recognize that, as they were growing up, they needed more independence. He resented every effort they made to craft their own lives separate from him. Susy longed to become a singer and Clara wanted a career as a pianist. Twain was annoyed by their ambitions. He paid for their music lessons, but only begrudgingly.

Despite his personal turmoil, Twain continued to write. In 1892, he published *The American Claimant*, a novel that revived the character Colonel Sellers, who was originally seen in *The Gilded Age*. Twain also wrote two new books about the popular Tom Sawyer—*Tom Sawyer Abroad* (1894) and *Tom Sawyer, Detective* (1896). In 1896, he also published what he regarded as one of his best works, *Personal Recollections of Joan of Arc*, which is little read today.

Much more popular with modern readers is his novel *Pudd'nhead Wilson and Those Extraordinary Twins* (1894). In this book, Twain returned to the pre–Civil-War era and rendered arguably his most savage attack on the institution of slavery. Although the book has numerous side plots, its core story deals with a slave named Roxy, who tries to save her light-skinned infant from enslavement by switching him at birth with the baby of her white owner. Roxy is one of the few fully realized female characters in Twain's major works.

DECLARING BANKRUPTCY

By 1893, Twain's money troubles turned into a complete financial crisis. He had borrowed some $200,000 through his publishing company, but he had poured much of the money into the Paige typesetter, which, despite Paige's assurances, still did not work well. Twain returned to the United States to find new investors to bail out Webster & Company, but that proved impossible. The country had fallen into a deep economic downturn, today known as the Panic of 1893. During this serious economic depression, unemployment rose, credit dried up, and anyone with enough money to invest held onto it, waiting for the financial outlook to improve.

The desperate Twain found help from an unlikely source. Henry H. Rogers, the vice president of Standard Oil, was a very rich and ruthless businessman, just like the ones Twain had lambasted in *The Gilded Age.* Rogers, however, was also a great fan of Twain's books. When he heard of Twain's money woes, he volunteered to help. He gave Twain a loan of $8,000 to keep the publishing house afloat and agreed to look at the author's finances and advise him about what he should do next.

Rogers's recommendation was not what Twain wanted to hear. He said Webster & Company had to declare bankruptcy. Rogers figured out a way to allow Twain to keep the Hartford house and to retain the copyrights to his books. But everything else was gone. Twain was horrified, in large part because he knew how Livy would respond. The bankruptcy would allow the company legally to renege on some of its debts. To Livy, this would be morally wrong and disgraceful. Hating to see Livy humiliated as a result of his bad investments, Twain declared he would pay back all his creditors, even though he was not required to by law.

TOURING THE WORLD

Throughout Twain's writing career, the lecture circuit was one surefire way he could make a great deal of money in a short period of time. The idea of lecturing again, however, filled him with horror. He had long hated the grind of constant traveling. Now, at 60, he doubted whether he had the physical stamina to do it again.

Yet, Twain had no other choice. In April 1895, he signed a contract to tour first in the northwestern United States, then in nations that were then part of the British Empire, including Australia, New Zealand, India, and South Africa. The family decided that Livy and Clara would come along. Susy and Jean would stay behind. Susy would live at her Aunt Susan's house to continue her vocal training. Jean, feeling too ill and frail to travel, would go to school in Elmira.

Twain's ambitious tour was a great success. His books now had a worldwide audience, so everywhere he went he was greeted by adoring crowds. His tour quickly proved more lucrative than he had expected. Each time he sent money back to Rogers, he felt more confident that his financial crisis and Livy's humiliation would be over soon.

Be good + you will be lonesome.

Mark Twain

In order to pay his creditors, Mark Twain embarked on a world tour and later recorded his experiences in Following the Equator *(1897). Here is he photographed aboard ship on his way around the world.*

The tour also allowed him to begin work on a new travel book, one he was sure would be a big seller. He took notes about seeing the famous Taj Mahal, riding an elephant in India, and visiting a diamond mine in South Africa. He later collected his impressions in *Following the Equator* (1897). In the book, Twain was highly critical of colonialism—the practice of one nation taking control of a weaker country's economic and political system. During the nineteenth century, many European countries were colonialist powers that sought dominance over areas in Asia and Africa. Twain was disgusted by the way the British treated the natives in the lands they colonized. He wrote:

> [I]n many countries we [white people] have taken the savage's land from him, and made him our slave, and lashed him every day, and broken his pride, and made death his only friend, and overworked him till he dropped in his tracks. . . . There are many humorous things in the world; among them the white man's notion that he is less savage than the other savages.[5]

His increasing revulsion with the exploitation of native peoples mirrored his evolving feelings about slavery. As a young boy, he never questioned slavery, but as he grew older he recognized it as a moral abomination. Similarly, as a young man, in works such as *Roughing It*, he supported the U.S. military's campaign of extermination against western Indian groups in order to take over their lands. When he matured, however, he recognized the injustice of this type of policy.

A DEATH IN THE FAMILY

In the summer of 1896, exhausted but heartened, Twain, Livy, and Clara set off for England. While they were pleased that the tour had paid off most of their debts, they were thrilled by the idea that they would soon see Susy and Jean again. They sent a cable to the girls, asking them to take the next ship from New York to London.

As they eagerly awaited their family reunion, they received a telegram. Susy was ill. A second soon arrived with the comforting news that, although she was facing a long recovery, Susy would be fine. Livy and Clara took the next ship to New York so they could care for Susy, while Twain stayed behind to work on his book and to find a suitable place where they all could live once Susy recovered.

On August 18, Twain received a third telegram. It said that Susy, at just 24, had died. While spending the summer in Hartford, she had contracted spinal meningitis, a viral or bacterial infection that causes an inflammation of the brain and spinal column. For weeks, her fevered brain made her delusional. She eventually lost her sight and lapsed into a coma before succumbing to her illness.

Twain was inconsolable. Left alone to cope with his overwhelming grief, he wrote Livy letter after letter, knowing his sorrowful words would be unread until she reached the port in New York. As he had when other loved ones had died, Twain found ample ways of blaming himself for the tragedy. If he had not been so careless with his fortune, his family would never have been separated. If his family had not been separated, he and Livy would have been there when Susy fell ill and could have nursed her back to health. He wrote to Livy, saying, "I have spent the day alone— thinking; sometimes bitter thoughts, sometimes only sad ones. Reproaching myself for laying the foundation of all our troubles. . . . Reproaching myself for a million things whereby I have brought misfortune and sorrow to this family."[6] Although Twain was always deeply affected by death, the loss of Susy was perhaps the greatest blow of his life. With Susy gone, there was never any hope of reclaiming those happy days in Hartford when, with his loving wife, his beautiful girls, and his unbelievable success, he had felt like the luckiest man in the world.

Mark Twain is shown with, from left, his daughter, Clara, and his wife, Olivia, at their suburban London home in 1900. The last years of the author's life would be filled with heartache.

The Final Years

AFTER LAYING SUSY to rest, Livy, Clara, and Jean traveled to England to be reunited with Twain. The family was together again, but the absence of Susy continued to cast a long shadow. Twain holed up in their rented home, trying to distract himself from his gnawing grief by writing. He was so seldom seen outside that a rumor spread that he was either dead or dying. A reporter assigned to find out arrived at the Twain's door. He told the still very much alive Twain that his editor had instructed him to write 500 words if Twain were sick and 1,000 words if he were dead. Twain replied, "You don't need as much as that. Just say the report of my death has been greatly exaggerated."[1]

IN VIENNA

In 1897, Twain once again uprooted his family. He decided they should relocate to Vienna, Austria. Clara desperately wanted to study piano with a teacher there, and although her parents were not pleased with her choice of career, they agreed to let her take lessons in Vienna. Unwilling to separate the family again, Twain moved the entire household there.

During his two years in Vienna, Twain was treated as a celebrity. Reporters came to his home to interview him, and artists begged him to pose for paintings and sculptures. Twain continued to write at a furious pace, sometimes working eight hours straight. He labored over numerous manuscripts at the same time, many of which he never intended to publish.

During this period, Twain produced one of his most famous stories, "The Man That Corrupted Hadleyburg." The story took him back to a town much like Hannibal, but this time the town and its inhabitants were more sinister than before. The man that "corrupts" Hadleyburg actually only reveals the self-righteousness and hypocrisy underlying the veneer of Christian decency among its leading citizens.

Twain also wrote an odd philosophical tract titled "What Is Man?" It argued that human beings are essentially machines, incapable of independent thought and therefore not responsible for their actions. In the essay, Twain suggested that human progress was impossible because people were unable to grow as moral beings. Because Livy hated the work, he agreed not to publish it during her lifetime.

GOING HOME

By the late 1890s, Twain had finally emerged from the black cloud of his bankruptcy. To Livy's relief, his lecture tour and books had earned enough to pay off all his debts. He even had some money left over, which he started investing in new get-rich-quick schemes. Among them was a product called Plasmon, a food supplement that promised to end world hunger.

Yet, just as one problem was solved, another emerged. Twain's youngest daughter, Jean, had always been sickly, but recently, especially after Susy's death, she began having violent seizures. In Europe, Jean was diagnosed with epilepsy, a serious neurological disorder. At the time, epilepsy was not only a dangerous illness but also a badge of shame.

Twain and Livy desperately sought a cure for Jean. They moved to Sweden, then England, in search of a doctor who could successfully treat her. In London, Jean's physicians told Twain that they could do nothing more for her than doctors in New York City could. After nine years of exile, Twain decided it was time to go home.

COURTING CONTROVERSY

Twain and his family arrived in New York in 1900. When their ship reached the harbor, reporters were waiting to greet the famed author. His years away from the United States had not diminished America's love for Mark Twain. In fact, his story of surviving bankruptcy and honoring his debts had endeared him even more to the American public.

No one in the family could stand the idea of going back to the Hartford house where Susy had died, so they rented a home in the city. There, Twain received a steady stream of visitors, including many journalists who came to rely on him for clever comments about the news of the day. He became more outspoken politically, especially in his criticisms of colonialism and imperialism. He spoke out against

Britain's actions in the Boer War in South Africa, the role of Christian missionaries in the Boxer Rebellion in China, and the Belgians' subjugation of the people of the Congo in Africa.

Twain was also critical of many U.S. policies, including the United States' military operations in the Philippines. In 1898, U.S. soldiers had arrived in the Philippines to help its people revolt against their Spanish rulers. But after the Spanish had relinquished control, the Americans began fighting the rebel Filipinos in order to take over their country. Deteriorating conditions for blacks in the American South also appalled Twain. He considered writing a book titled "The United States of Lyncherdom," in which he intended to attack the bigoted Southern whites who were terrorizing African Americans to keep them from enjoying their basic civil rights. He eventually abandoned the project, probably because he was afraid Southerners would turn against him and his family. In general, however, his strong political views had almost no effect on his popularity.

LOSING LIVY

Livy began having heart trouble and asthma attacks after the Twains moved to a large house in the Bronx, New York. Her doctors confined her to her bedroom and forbade Twain from visiting her for more than a few minutes each day. They believed his volatile temperament would upset their patient and slow her recovery. In truth, Livy's separation from her husband proved incredibly stressful to her. Her happiest moments were when a servant delivered letters from Twain, who wrote to her two or three times a day. Once, he amused her by hanging notes on a tree outside her window that instructed birds not to sing too loudly, lest they disturb his lovely wife.

Clara Clemens was a contralto concert singer and Mark Twain's only surviving daughter. After his death in 1910, she managed his estate and guarded his legacy.

Seeking a better climate for Livy, Twain moved the family to Florence, Italy, in 1903. During the spring of 1904, she seemed to be getting better. On June 5, she appeared so healthy that he spent a full half hour in her room. After he left, he began playing the piano and singing old African-American spirituals he had learned as a child. Listening to her husband's voice ring out from a nearby room, Livy Clemens died. Her death was devastating to Twain and his daughters. Their longtime housekeeper, Katy Leary, later recalled their reaction: "Oh, he cried all that time, and Clara and Jean. They put their arms around their father's neck and they cried, the three of them, as though their hearts would break."[2]

Shattered by the loss of her mother, Clara had a mental collapse and checked herself into a sanitarium. Jean began having more seizures and acted so erratically that Twain committed her to a mental hospital against her wishes. Twain returned to New York City, where his household came to include Isabel Lyon, his secretary; and Albert Bigelow Paine, his official biographer.

LONELY DAYS

Twain continued to write, spending much of his time on his autobiography. He did not want to create a standard autobiography that started with his birth and moved chronologically through the events of his life. Instead, Twain tried to recreate the genre by telling stories out of order and mixing letters, essays, and newspaper clippings into the narrative. Often dictating the work to Lyon, he produced an enormous amount of material, only a fraction of which would be published during his life.

Twain's final years were his loneliest. Although Clara returned home, she wanted little to do with her demanding father. He instead looked for companionship from Lyon and Paine, who were more fawning admirers than friends. He also sought out the company of young girls from neighboring families, perhaps because they reminded him of a time when his own daughters lavished him with affection and adoration. He called his young friends "angel fish."

Twain also enjoyed the admiration of his readers. He took to walking through the streets of New York on Sundays just as church let out to attract crowds of fans. To make sure they saw him, he wore a white suit and red socks. Twain also enjoyed attending fancy banquets, many of which were held in his honor. In elite New York society, Twain was a welcome guest. Dinner hosts could expect him to deliver a charming and amusing speech if asked, as he always was.

STORMFIELD

In 1907, Twain, wanting a home of his own, hired architect John Howells, the son of his friend William Dean Howells,

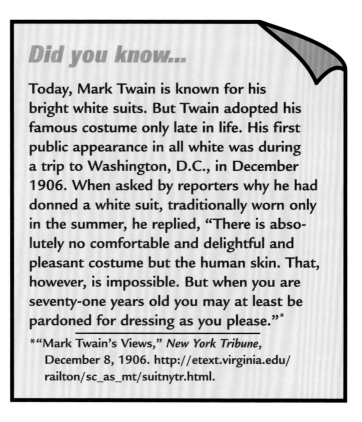

Did you know...

Today, Mark Twain is known for his bright white suits. But Twain adopted his famous costume only late in life. His first public appearance in all white was during a trip to Washington, D.C., in December 1906. When asked by reporters why he had donned a white suit, traditionally worn only in the summer, he replied, "There is absolutely no comfortable and delightful and pleasant costume but the human skin. That, however, is impossible. But when you are seventy-one years old you may at least be pardoned for dressing as you please."*

*"Mark Twain's Views," *New York Tribune*, December 8, 1906. http://etext.virginia.edu/ railton/sc_as_mt/suitnytr.html.

A portrait of Mark Twain in his later years. Although he was beloved worldwide for his wit and wisdom, the deaths of his wife and daughter Jean brought a profound change in him.

to design a house on land he had purchased near Redding, Connecticut. When he moved in the following year, he dubbed the house "Stormfield" after a character in a story he was working on. Lyon, who supervised Stormfield's construction, took on the role of the lady of the house.

In July 1909, the *New York Herald* announced a rumor that Twain and Lyon were engaged. The rumor was untrue, but probably to squelch any more, Lyon married Twain's business manager, Ralph Ashcroft. Clara, who was deeply suspicious of Lyon and Ashcroft, was convinced they were trying to get their hands on Twain's money. Twain ceded to Clara's demands that he fire them and remove them from his life.

In October 1909, Clara and pianist Ossip Gabrilowitsch were married on the lawn of Stormfield. Always needing to be the center of attention, even at his daughter's wedding, Twain wore the red and gray robe he was given by Oxford University, when it awarded him an honorary doctorate in 1907. Clara and her husband immediately left for Europe, but by that time Twain had allowed Jean to rejoin his household. The two developed a new and deep affection for each other. Twain wrote, "Jean is a surprise and a wonder. She has plenty of wisdom, judgment, penetration, practical good sense—like her mother."[3]

That year, Jean hoped to make Christmas special for her father. She set up a Christmas tree and decorated the house as her parents had when she was young. The holiday, however, was destined to be far from merry. On the morning of Christmas Eve, Jean had a seizure while bathing. She died either of a heart attack caused by the seizure or by drowning.

Twain, his own health failing, was too frail and distraught to attend her funeral. Yet he soon set off for the island of Bermuda, where he had taken to going in the harshest months of winter. By March, his doctors told him he was dying. He managed to return to Stormfield, where he was joined by Clara and her husband. On the night of April 21, 1910, Mark Twain died in his bed with his only surviving daughter holding his hand.

Mark Twain's popularity has continued to grow since his death in 1910. In this circa 1955 photo, the old riverboat pilot wheel of Captain Samuel Clemens is shown at a commemorative museum in the author's hometown of Hannibal, Missouri.

8

The Legacy of Mark Twain

LEARNING OF MARK TWAIN'S death, newspapers all over the world bore banner headlines, informing their readers of the sad news. After recapping his career and singing his praises, many obituaries turned to another topic—just how history would remember Mark Twain. For instance, the *New York Times* explained, "That Samuel L. Clemens was the greatest American humorist of his age nobody will deny," before pondering whether his work would one day be forgotten. After all, the paper argued, Twain's onetime mentor Artemus Ward had been "Mark Twain's greatest predecessor as a National jester," but by the time of Twain's death was "little more than a name."

The obituary concluded that no matter the fate of Twain's writings, his celebrity would always be remembered:

> His death will be mourned, everywhere, and smiles will break through the tears as remembrance of the man's rich gift to his era comes to the mourners' minds. However his work may be judged by impartial and unprejudiced generations his fame is imperishable.[1]

THE MYSTERIOUS STRANGER

One person was determined to preserve the legacy of both Twain the man and Twain the author. As his official biographer, Albert Bigelow Paine had lived with Twain during his final years. Upon Twain's death, he became the author's literary executor—the person in charge of deciding what to do with a deceased writer's published and unpublished works. In the case of Twain, the amount of unpublished works left behind was enormous. Paine was given control over more than 500 unpublished and unfinished manuscripts, including that of Twain's massive and unwieldy autobiography.

In addition to his three-volume biography published in 1912, Paine, with the help of Twain's daughter Clara, prepared several new Twain books for publication. He collected a volume of Twain's letters and edited portions of his autobiography. Paine's editing, however, has since been severely criticized by Twain scholars. He cut out anything he thought was controversial or that he feared would color the image of the great Mark Twain.

Paine's most notorious case of editorial meddling was a book titled *The Mysterious Stranger: A Romance.* With the help of Frederick A. Duneka, an editor at Harper &

Brothers, Paine took an unfinished work titled "The Chronicle of Young Satan" and tacked on an ending from an unpublished novel, "No. 44, The Mysterious Stranger." Paine and Duneka then rewrote many passages, added an entirely new character, and edited out anything they thought might offend Christian readers. This strange amalgamation was published in 1916 and marketed as a Christmas gift book for children. For decades, *The Mysterious Stranger: A Romance* confounded Twain fans and scholars, who struggled to understand this largely incoherent work. Not until the 1960s did Twain expert John Tuckey reveal the extent of Paine and Duneka's editing. Although they had more hand in creating this work than Twain, editions of the book listing Twain as its author are still available.

REEXAMINING TWAIN

After Paine's death in 1937, a series of far more responsible executors took over the Twain literary estate. Clara still resisted the publication of Twain's late works, but after her death in 1962, the estate published several books that have become important in the Twain canon, including *Letters from the Earth* (1962) and *Mark Twain's Which Was the Dream? and Other Symbolic Writings of the Later Years* (1967). Biographers of Twain also became more willing to explore his dark side. Hamlin Hill's *Mark Twain: God's Fool* (1973) was especially influential in its frank examination of Twain's flagging spirit at the end of his life. Although some scholars have challenged the bleakness of Hill's depiction of the aging Twain, the book helped encourage a more balanced view of Twain than his first executor had allowed.

Far from diminishing his stature, such reexaminations of Twain and his work have enhanced his literary reputation. During his lifetime, friends and fans of Twain feared he would be remembered, if at all, as merely a humorist. But not long after his death, Twain was heralded by several vocal and influential fans. The respected journalist, essayist, and critic H.L. Mencken, for instance, was a great champion of Twain's work. In a 1913 essay titled "The Burden of Humor," he wrote, "[Mark Twain is] the noblest literary artist, who ever set pen to paper on American soil, and not only the noblest artist, but also one of the most profound and sagacious philosophers."[2] Ernest Hemingway, regarded as one of the best American authors of the twentieth century, also offered high praise for Twain. In his book *Green Hills of Africa* (1935), Hemingway claimed, "All modern American literature comes from one book by Mark Twain called *Huckleberry Finn*."[3]

In the years following World War II (1939–1945), Twain's literary standing continued to grow. In colleges and universities, the student bodies swelled by returning veterans, interest in American literature increased. Twain, with his laserlike examinations of everything good and bad in the American character, naturally became an important part of the college and high school curricula. Today, Twain is so commonly taught that it is hard to imagine a serious student of American literature not being assigned at least one of his works.

Recent decades have also seen an explosion of scholarly interest in Twain's writing. As a result, experts have reevaluated his works, often coming to view them very differently than they had been seen during Twain's lifetime. For instance, in his day, Twain was best known as a travel writer. Although *Innocents Abroad* and *Roughing It* are still widely read, Twain is now much better known as a novelist. His political works have also become more popular. Controversial when he wrote them, Twain's critiques of colonialism and imperialism are now much more in tune with modern opinion.

RETHINKING *HUCKLEBERRY FINN*

Perhaps the most significant development in Twain studies is the elevation of *Adventures of Huckleberry Finn*. The novel originally sold fairly well, but it was far from Twain's greatest success with readers or with critics. Today, *Huckleberry Finn* is hailed as his masterpiece. When it was published, its depiction of slavery was hardly remarked upon. But for modern readers, it is considered one of the most important books about race ever published by an American author.

Some of Twain's contemporaries charged that the book's language was vulgar, a complaint seldom heard now. *Huckleberry Finn*'s strongest detractors today generally attack it for its use of a single derogatory term, long used as an insulting word for a black person, which is deeply offensive to African Americans. Throughout *Huckleberry Finn*, Jim is frequently called this racial slur, just as a slave certainly would have been in the time Twain depicts. But many critics claim that, even if historically accurate, repeated use of the word is insulting to African-American readers. Some also cite it as evidence that Twain himself was a racist. As a result of these concerns, *Huckleberry Finn* is one of the books most often banned in American high school classrooms and libraries.

In recent years, others have charged that, because of its ending, *Huckleberry Finn* is a fundamentally racist work.

As previously mentioned, in its final chapters, Tom Sawyer and Huck Finn play a trick on Jim, convincing him he is still enslaved while they know he has been set free. Twain's first audiences thought of the episode as a fun, boyish prank. Later readers, however, have been appalled by Tom and Huck's behavior. How could Twain depict Jim with such humanity earlier in the book, only to turn around and have his young characters treat Jim like a toy for their own amusement?

Some critics of the ending, including Hemingway, contend that Twain just made a horrible mistake as a writer. Unable to figure out how to end the book, he panicked and resorted to what he saw as crowd-pleasing comedy. Others charge that, at the core, Twain just did not really care that much about his most famous African-American character. For instance, in her 1996 essay "Say It Ain't So, Huck: Reflections on Mark Twain's 'Masterpiece'," Pulitzer Prize–winning novelist Jane Smiley argued that in the end, neither Twain nor Huck were able to fully respect Jim and his passionate desire to be free.

HUCKLEBERRY FINN AND RECONSTRUCTION

Some Twain fans, however, interpret the ending not as a creative failure, but as a commentary on his own times. The year he began *Huckleberry Finn*, 1876, marked the beginning of the end of Reconstruction. Reconstruction, which lasted from 1865 to 1877, was a collection of federal policies designed to help rebuild the South after the Civil War. Many of these policies focused on helping ex-slaves integrate into American society as free people. When the U.S. government ended Reconstruction and federal troops no longer occupied Southern states, these states moved quickly to strip blacks of their rights. Through what were nicknamed Jim Crow laws, they denied African Americans the right to vote, own property, and live where they chose. While Twain was writing *Huckleberry Finn*, Southern blacks were being forced into an impoverished, dependent state that left them little better off than they had been under slavery.

Some readers have concluded that Twain's ending is a condemnation of what was happening in the South. Like Jim at the end of *Huckleberry Finn*, Southern blacks were technically free, but they were not able to act on that freedom. In this reading, the boys' unkind prank on Jim is a metaphor for Jim Crow laws. One admirer of the book, the renowned African-American writer Ralph Ellison, maintained that Hemingway (and by extension other white readers) had failed to grasp this as the very point of Twain's novel:

> So thoroughly had the Negro . . . been pushed into the underground of the American conscience that Hemingway missed completely the structural, symbolic, and moral necessity for that part of the plot in which the boys rescue Jim. Yet it is precisely this part that gives the novel its significance. Without it, except as a boy's tale, the novel is meaningless.[4]

Because of the debate over *Huckleberry Finn* and the strong emotions it inspires, some schools prefer to teach Twain's other great novel about race, *Pudd'nhead Wilson and Those Extraordinary Twins*. In this latter book, Twain is more direct in his criticism of racial discrimination and the pernicious effect slavery had on both the slave and the slave owner. *A Connecticut Yankee* has also become popular in the classroom. Once seen as a celebration of

The American actor Hal Holbrook has been well regarded for his impersonation of Mark Twain. Here he stands at a podium in a scene from the television production of the one-man play Mark Twain Tonight!, *directed by Paul Bogart and adapted by Holbrook.*

American ingenuity, it is now often taught as a critique of the Western world's eagerness to bring "civilization" to so-called primitive peoples, often only to destroy their societies in the process.

PLAYING MARK TWAIN

Today, Mark Twain is certainly one of the best-known American authors, but he is familiar not only to readers and scholars. Many people who have never read a word he wrote still know who he was, or, more accurately, is. Samuel Clemens died in 1910, but Mark Twain—arguably Clemens's greatest character—lives on.

The Mark Twain people know best was the persona he created at the end of his life—the wise old man with the white hair and the white suit, always with a lit cigar in his hand and a clever remark on his lips. Even while Twain was alive, much to his annoyance, a number of actors made their living as Twain impersonators. Hundreds of impersonators now work in the United States. They perform in theaters, at country fairs, at grocery store openings, or just about anywhere a crowd might be gathered.

The most accomplished Mark Twain impersonator is Hal Holbrook. This actor first performed as Twain in 1954, when he developed a nightclub show based on Twain's writings. He eventually took the show to the Broadway stage. His performance of *Mark Twain Tonight!* was nationally televised in 1967. For more than 50 years, Holbrook has toured with the show off and on, performing it more than 2,000 times. He has some 12 hours of Twain material committed to memory, which allows him to adapt the program to his audiences and to the events of the day.

Mark Twain is also still a popular pitchman. When he was alive, he was not above appearing in advertisements, particularly after he copyrighted his pen name so that he would receive fees from the companies whose products he hawked. In his own day, Twain was used to selling whiskey, tobacco, cigars, and shirt collars. More recently, he has appeared in advertisements for beer and fountain pens. Products featuring Twain's face are also popular items. Fans can purchase T-shirts, calendars, and even statues bearing Twain's image.

TWAIN IN ENTERTAINMENT

Given Twain's popularity as a performer, it seems appropriate that, a century after his death, he remains a force in the entertainment industry. Over the years, Twain has "guest starred" in a number of television shows, including *Bonanza*, *Cheers*, *Star Trek: The Next Generation*, *Sabrina the Teenage Witch*, and *Touched by an Angel*. He has also been a featured performer at the Walt Disney World theme park in Florida. For years, an animatronic Twain has offered park visitors his take on American history.

In addition to Mark Twain the character, movies and television have also embraced Mark Twain the author. The first filmed version of a Twain work was *The Prince and the Pauper*, a 1909 movie produced by inventor Thomas Edison. Twain played himself in the film. Since that time, audiences have enjoyed dozens of screen adaptations of Twain's books. Just a few produced since 1990 include a Disney feature film titled *Tom and Huck*; *A Million to Juan*, a version of his story "The £1,000,000 Bank-Note" tailored for Mexican-American star and director Paul Rodriguez; a television movie of *Roughing It* starring James Garner as

Twain; a direct-to-DVD movie with an animated Barbie doll playing a princess and a pauper; and a short film dramatizing Twain's antiwar short story "The War Prayer" as a commentary on the Iraq War.

In addition to Hal Holbrook's show, Twain and his works have also made frequent appearances onstage. The most famous theater piece inspired by a Twain book is *Big River*. Based on *Huckleberry Finn*, the show won the 1985 Tony Award for Best Musical. In 2003, Twain's own play *Is He Dead?* made its world premiere on Broadway. Discovered in 2002, it had been written by Twain in 1898 but had never before been performed.

In the world of literature, there have been numerous contemporary novels published featuring Twain's characters. Twain himself has often made appearances in popular

Did you know...

In 1998, the John F. Kennedy Center for the Performing Arts in Washington, D.C., announced an annual award to honor comedians who have had an important impact on American society and culture. Not surprisingly, the organization called it the Mark Twain Prize, after perhaps the most beloved American humorist of all time. Among the recipients of the Mark Twain Prize have been Richard Pryor, Whoopi Goldberg, George Carlin, Lily Tomlin, Bill Cosby, and Tina Fey.

fiction as a character in other writers' historical novels, detective stories, romances, and even science fiction.

TWAIN IN OUR TIMES

Even Americans who never turn on a television, go to the movies, or crack open a novel are likely to run into the words "Mark Twain." Throughout the United States, there are hundreds of institutions and businesses that bear his name. There are Mark Twain banks, Mark Twain hotels, Mark Twain restaurants, and, in Missouri, even a Mark Twain national forest. Schools named after Twain dot the country—from Brooklyn, New York; to Alvin, Texas; to San Diego, California.

For Twain enthusiasts, there are also several museums devoted to the author. His beloved home in Hartford, Connecticut, has been preserved as the Mark Twain House & Museum. Twain's boyhood house in Hannibal, Missouri, is also open to the public. Hannibal further capitalizes on its connection to Twain through steamboat rides and other Twain-related tourist attractions. The town named 2010 "the year of Mark Twain"[5] in commemoration of the one-hundredth anniversary of Twain's death.

In *A Connecticut Yankee*, Twain had his protagonist, Hank Morgan, travel back in time to medieval England—possibly the first example of time travel in American fiction. What would happen if Twain were able to make a similar trip to twenty-first century America? What would he make of schools named after him, movies adapted from his books, and T-shirts emblazoned with his face? It is easy to assume he would be pleased. After all, he spent much of his life crafting and honing the persona of Mark Twain. Most likely, he would be delighted to see that, a century after his death, Twain was still alive and kicking. But Samuel Clemens would probably be most gratified, and most surprised, to see the many classrooms full of students debating his works. He passionately wanted his writing to live on, and live on it did.

CHRONOLOGY

1835 Samuel Langhorne Clemens is born in Florida, Missouri, on November 30.

1839 Moves with family to Hannibal, Missouri.

1847 Father John Clemens dies.

1850 Goes to work for elder brother Orion's newspaper.

1853 Leaves Hannibal to work as a printer in St. Louis, New York, and Philadelphia.

1855 Reunites with family in Keokuk, Iowa.

1857 Becomes an apprentice to riverboat pilot Horace Bixby.

1861 Piloting career ends with the outbreak of the Civil War; serves briefly in the Confederate militia; moves to Nevada Territory with Orion.

1862 Becomes a reporter for the *Territorial Enterprise* in Virginia City.

1863 Uses the pen name Mark Twain for the first time.

1864 Begins working for newspapers in San Francisco, California.

1865 Writes "Jim Smiley and His Jumping Frog," which is published in the *New York Saturday Press*.

1866 Writes travel letters about the Sandwich Islands (now Hawaii); delivers first public lecture in San Francisco.

1867 Travels to Europe and the Middle East aboard the *Quaker City*.

1869 Becomes engaged to Olivia Langdon; the best-selling *Innocents Abroad*, based on his travel letters from the *Quaker City* trip, is published.

1870 Marries Olivia Langdon in Elmira, New York; son Langdon is born.

1871 Moves family to Hartford, Connecticut.

1872 Daughter Susy is born; son Langdon dies.

1874 Daughter Clara is born; work begins on the Mark Twain House in Hartford, Connecticut.

1876 *The Adventures of Tom Sawyer* is published.

1880 Daughter Jean is born.

1883 *Life on the Mississippi* is published.

1884 Establishes publishing firm Webster & Company; publishes *Adventures of Huckleberry Finn* in December.

1889 *A Connecticut Yankee in King Arthur's Court* is published.

1891–1895 Travels through Europe with his family.

1894 Declares bankruptcy of Webster & Company after losing a fortune through bad investments.

1895 Begins world lecture tour in order to pay off his debts.

1896 Daughter Susy dies.

1902 Visits Hannibal for the last time.

1903 Moves family to Florence, Italy.

1904 Olivia dies; returns to New York City.

1907 Receives honorary degree from Oxford University in England.

1908 Moves to new house, Stormfield, in Redding, Connecticut.

1909 Clara marries Ossip Gabrilowitsch; Jean dies.

1910 Dies at Stormfield on April 21 at the age of 74.

1912 Albert Bigelow Paine's three-volume biography of Twain is published.

1916 *The Mysterious Stranger: A Romance* is published.

1954 Actor Hal Holbrook premieres one-man show in which he impersonates Twain.

1962 *Letters from the Earth* is published; Mark Twain's papers are bequeathed to the University of California.

1963 The Mark Twain House in Hartford is declared a National Historic Landmark.

1985 *Big River*, based on *Huckleberry Finn*, wins the Tony Award for Best Musical.

1986 The Mark Twain Circle of America is established.

1997 Oxford University Press publishes the 29-volume Oxford Mark Twain collection.

2010 World celebrates Twain on the one-hundredth anniversary of his death.

NOTES

Chapter 1

1 Gary Scharnhorst, ed., *Mark Twain: The Complete Interviews.* Tuscaloosa: University of Alabama Press, 2006, p. 418.

2 Ibid.

3 Ibid., p. 419.

4 Ibid., p. 420.

5 Ibid., p. 413.

6 Ibid., p. 412.

7 Ibid., p. 413.

8 Ibid., p. 428.

9 Ibid., p. 429.

10 Ibid., p. 427.

11 Ibid., p. 465.

12 Ibid., p. 440.

13 Ibid., p. 465.

14 Ron Powers, *Mark Twain: A Life.* New York: Free Press, 2005, p. 613.

15 Scharnhorst, p. 457.

16 Ibid., p. 459.

17 Ibid., p. 452.

Chapter 2

1 Geoffrey C. Ward, Dayton Duncan, and Ken Burns, *Mark Twain: An Illustrated Biography.* New York: Alfred A. Knopf, 2001, pp. 3–4.

2 Ibid., p. 4.

3 Ibid., p. 11.

4 Gregg Camfield, *The Oxford Companion to Mark Twain.* New York: Oxford University Press, 2003, p. 114.

5 Ibid., p. 116.

6 Ward et al, p. 14.

Chapter 3

1 Ward et al, p. 18.

2 Ibid., p. 30.

3 Ibid., p. 36.

4 Ibid., p. 48.

5 Ibid., p. 54.

6 Ibid.

Chapter 4

1 Ward et al, p. 55.

2 Ibid., p. 60.

3 Stephen Railton, *Mark Twain: A Short Introduction.* Malden, Mass.: Blackwell Publishing, 2004, pp. 4–5.

4 Ward et al, p. 77.

5 Ibid., p. 79.

6 Ibid., p. 81.

7 Ibid., p. 78.

8 Mark Twain, *The Innocents Abroad, or the New Pilgrims' Progress.* Hartford, Conn.: American Publishing Company, 1869, p. 486.

9 Ward et al, p. 78.

10 Ibid., p. 88.

Chapter 5

1 Ward et al, p. 86.

2 Camfield, p. 528.

3 Ward et al, p. 93.

4 Ibid., p. 96.

5 Railton, p. 38.

6 Ward et al, p. 117.

7 Mark Twain, *Adventures of Huckleberry Finn.* 1885. Reprint, New York: Harper & Brothers, 1912, p. 297.

8 Railton, p. 66.

9 Ibid.

10 Ibid.

11 Ward et al, p. 122.

12 Ibid., p. 123.

13 Ibid.

14 Ibid., p. 124.

Chapter 6

1 Ward et al, p. 143.

2 Railton, p. 90.

3 Mark Twain, *A Connecticut Yankee in King Arthur's Court.* 1889. Reprint, New York: Harper & Brothers, 1917, p. 108.

4 Railton, p. 82.

5 Ward et al, p. 174.

6 Ibid., p. 177.

Chapter 7

1 Ward et al, p. 188.

2 Ibid., p. 219.

3 Ibid., p. 249.

Chapter 8

1 "Mark Twain Is Dead at 74," *New York Times*, April 22, 1910. http://etext.virginia.edu/railton/sc_as_mt/mtobit8.html.

2 Camfield, p. 142.

3 Railton, p. 50.

4 Shelley Fisher Fishkin, *Lighting Out for the Territory: Reflections on Mark Twain and American Culture.* New York: Oxford University Press, 1996, p. 198.

5 Hannibal Convention & Visitors Bureau, "The Year of Mark Twain 2010." http://www.twain2010.org.

WORKS BY MARK TWAIN

1867 *The Celebrated Jumping Frog of Calaveras County, and Other Sketches*

1869 *The Innocents Abroad, or The New Pilgrims' Progress*

1871 *Mark Twain's (Burlesque) Autobiography and First Romance*

1872 *Roughing It*

1873 *The Gilded Age: A Tale of Today* (co-authored with Charles Dudley Warner)

1875 *Mark Twain's Sketches, New and Old*

1876 *The Adventures of Tom Sawyer*; *Ah Sin* (co-authored with Bret Harte)

1877 *A True Story and the Recent Carnival of Crime*

1878 *Punch, Brothers, Punch!*

1880 *A Tramp Abroad*; *1601, or Conversation as It Was by the Social Fireside in the Time of the Tudors*

1882 *The Stolen White Elephant Etc.*; *The Prince and the Pauper*

1883 *Life on the Mississippi*

1884 *Adventures of Huckleberry Finn*

1889 *A Connecticut Yankee in King Arthur's Court*

1892 *Merry Tales*; *The American Claimant*

1893 *The £1,000,000 Bank-Note and Other New Stories*

1894 *Tom Sawyer Abroad*; *Pudd'nhead Wilson and Those Extraordinary Twins*

1896 *Personal Recollections of Joan of Arc*; *Tom Sawyer, Detective*

1897 *How to Tell a Story and Other Essays*; *Following the Equator: A Journey Around the World*

1900 "The Man That Corrupted Hadleyburg"; *English as She Is Taught*

1901 *To the Person Sitting in Darkness*

1902 *A Double-Barrelled Detective Story*

1903 *My Debut as a Literary Person with Other Essays and Stories*

1904 *Extracts from Adam's Diary, Translated from the Original MS; A Dog's Tale*

1905 *King Leopold's Soliloquy*

1906 *What Is Man?; Eve's Diary; The $30,000 Bequest*

1907 *Christian Science with Notes Containing Corrections to Date; A Horse's Tale*

1909 *Is Shakespeare Dead?*

1910 *Mark Twain's Speeches*

1916 *The Mysterious Stranger: A Romance*

1917 *What Is Man? And Other Essays*

1923 *Europe and Elsewhere*

1924 *Mark Twain's Autobiography*

1940 *Mark Twain in Eruption*

1952 *Report from Paradise*

1957 *Mark Twain of the* Enterprise

1959 *The Autobiography of Mark Twain*

1962 *Letters from the Earth*

1967 *Mark Twain's "Which Was the Dream?" and Other Symbolic Writings of the Later Years*

1969 *Mark Twain's Mysterious Stranger Manuscripts*

1972 *Mark Twain's Fables of Man*

1979 *Mark Twain's Notebooks & Journals* (3 vols.)

1981 *Early Tales & Sketches* (2 vols.)

1982 *No. 44, The Mysterious Stranger*

1992 *Collected Tales, Sketches, Speeches, and Essays* (2 vols.)

2002 *Mark Twain's Letters* (6 vols.)

2003 *Is He Dead? A Comedy in Three Acts*

2004 *Mark Twain's Helpful Hints for Good Living*

2009 *Who Is Mark Twain?*

2010 *The Autobiography of Mark Twain, Vol. 1*

POPULAR BOOKS

ADVENTURES OF HUCKLEBERRY FINN

An uneducated boy from Missouri, Huck Finn runs away from his drunken father. During his escape, he encounters Jim, a runaway slave. Together, the two travel the Mississippi River on a raft. Their time together and their adventures on shore lead Huck to reevaluate his beliefs and his society.

THE ADVENTURES OF TOM SAWYER

Tom Sawyer is a mischievous boy with a vivid imagination living on the Missouri frontier in the early nineteenth century. Over the course of a summer, Sawyer has a series of adventures involving his friend Huckleberry Finn, his would-be sweetheart Becky Thatcher, and a villainous murderer named Injun Joe.

A CONNECTICUT YANKEE IN KING ARTHUR'S COURT

In 1879, factory supervisor Hank Morgan is knocked unconscious and wakes up in sixth-century England. Distressed by the poverty and brutality of the medieval world, he tries to improve his new society by introducing it to nineteenth-century technology with catastrophic results.

THE INNOCENTS ABROAD

In his first travel book, Mark Twain describes a trip through Europe and the Middle East as a member of an American tour group. Blending fact and fiction, Twain's anecdotes poke fun at Old World pretensions and the behavior of his fellow travelers.

LETTERS FROM THE EARTH

In this collection of essays and stories, published more than 50 years after his death, Twain muses about religion and God. The title story is composed of letters written by Satan, in which he describes mankind to the archangels Gabriel and Michael.

LIFE ON THE MISSISSIPPI

Life on the Mississippi is part memoir and part travelogue. In the first section, Twain recalls his life as a young riverboat pilot in the years leading up to the Civil War. In the second section, he recounts his experiences during a trip to the Mississippi in 1882.

THE PRINCE AND THE PAUPER

In sixteenth-century England, Prince Edward and a young pauper named Tom Canty exchange identities. Through the experience, Tom-as-Edward learns about the responsibilities of leadership, while Edward-as-Tom discovers the struggles of the poor.

PUDD'NHEAD WILSON AND THOSE EXTRAORDINARY TWINS

In a Mississippi River town, a beautiful slave named Roxy exchanges her baby boy for her master's infant son. Twenty years later, the deception plays a role in a sensational murder trial, during which the title character, a lawyer the town has deemed a "pudd'nhead," proves not so stupid after all.

ROUGHING IT

Twain recounts his rollicking adventures in the West in the 1860s, during which he prospected for gold, worked as a timberman, and speculated in real estate before discovering his calling as a writer and lecturer.

POPULAR CHARACTERS

BECKY THATCHER

Based on Twain's first girlfriend, Becky Thatcher is the pretty girl with blonde hair who catches Tom Sawyer's fancy. Twain's most famous female character, she is best remembered for a dramatic episode in which she and Tom are trapped together in a cave in *The Adventures of Tom Sawyer*.

COLONEL ESCHOL SELLERS

Colonel Sellers made his debut in *The Gilded Age*, Twain's first novel, and then was revived for *The American Claimant*. An amiable, low-level con man, Sellers embraces a series of get-rich-quick schemes, which he always optimistically predicts will reap him millions.

DAVID "PUDD'NHEAD" WILSON

At 25, Easterner David Wilson arrives in Dawson's Landing, Missouri. He immediately makes a clever joke that goes over the townspeople's heads, so they brand him a "pudd'nhead"—a fool. In the novel that bears his name, through his talents as a lawyer, he shows himself to be the smartest man in town.

HANK MORGAN

One of Twain's most complex characters, Hank Morgan is a Connecticut factory supervisor until he finds himself in medieval England through the miracle of time travel. Confident and practical, he sets out to improve this world with his technological know-how, but he fails to predict the havoc his meddling will cause.

HUCKLEBERRY FINN

A secondary character in *The Adventures of Tom Sawyer*, Huckleberry Finn was so compelling to Twain that he gave him his own book. In *Adventures of Huckleberry Finn*, this ignorant boy from a small Missouri town is allowed to tell his own story, creating the first American novel written in vernacular language.

JIM

The moral force in *Huckleberry Finn*, Jim is an escaped slave whom Huck is persuaded to help in his bid for freedom. Through his friendship with the compassionate and loyal Jim, Huck comes to question the idea that blacks are inferior to whites and that slavery is a good and natural institution.

MARK TWAIN

In popular works such as *The Innocents Abroad*, Samuel Clemens presents himself as Mark Twain, a naïve character who still manages to expose the pretensions of others. As a performer on the lecture circuit, Clemens similarly masked himself as Twain, through whom he could safely voice uncomfortable truths.

TOM SAWYER

Modeled closely on Twain as a boy, Tom Sawyer is possibly the author's most famous creation. To readers worldwide, he has long been a symbol of youthful exuberance and gentle rebellion. Although always seeking approval and attention, Sawyer charmingly bends society's rules in his quest for adventure and fortune.

MAJOR AWARDS

1888 Twain receives an Honorary Master of Arts from Yale University.

1901 Twain receives an Honorary Doctor of Literature from Yale University.

1902 Twain receives an Honorary Doctor of Law from University of Missouri.

1907 Twain receives an Honorary Doctor of Letters from Oxford University.

BIBLIOGRAPHY

Camfield, Gregg. *The Oxford Companion to Mark Twain.* New York: Oxford University Press, 2003.

Fishkin, Shelley Fisher. *Lighting Out for the Territory: Reflections on Mark Twain and American Culture.* New York: Oxford University Press, 1996.

Lystra, Karen. *Dangerous Intimacy: The Untold Story of Mark Twain's Final Years.* Berkeley: University of California Press, 2004.

Messent, Peter. *The Cambridge Introduction to Mark Twain.* New York: Cambridge University Press, 2007.

Powers, Ron. *Mark Twain: A Life.* New York: Free Press, 2005.

Railton, Stephen. *Mark Twain: A Short Introduction.* Malden, Mass.: Blackwell Publishing, 2004.

Rasmussen, R. Kent. *Mark Twain A to Z: The Essential Reference to His Life and Writings.* New York: Facts on File, 1995.

Scharnhorst, Gary, ed. *Mark Twain: The Complete Interviews.* Tuscaloosa: University of Alabama Press, 2006.

Steinbrink, Jeffrey. *Getting to Be Mark Twain.* Berkeley: University of California Press, 1991.

Ward, Geoffrey C., Dayton Duncan, and Ken Burns. *Mark Twain: An Illustrated Biography.* New York: Alfred A. Knopf, 2001.

Ziff, Larzer. *Mark Twain.* New York: Oxford University Press, 2004.

FURTHER READING

Books

Aller, Susan Bivin. *Mark Twain.* Minneapolis, Minn.: Lerner Publications, 2006.

Bloom, Harold, ed. *Mark Twain.* New York: Chelsea House, 1999.

Cox, Clinton. *Mark Twain: America's Humorist, Dreamer, Prophet.* New York: Scholastic, 1995.

Fleischman, Sid. *The Trouble Begins at 8: A Life of Mark Twain in the Wild, Wild West.* New York: Greenwillow Books, 2008.

Houle, Michelle M. *Mark Twain: Banned, Challenged, and Censored.* Berkeley Heights, N.J.: Enslow Publishers, 2008.

Vickers, Rebecca. *The Story Behind Mark Twain's Adventures of Huckleberry Finn.* Chicago: Heinemann-Raintree, 2007.

Web Sites

The Mark Twain Boyhood Home & Museum
http://www.marktwainmuseum.org

Mark Twain in His Times
http://etext.lib.virginia.edu/railton/index2.html

The Mark Twain House & Museum
http://www.marktwainhouse.org

Mark Twain at Large: His Travels Here and Abroad
http://bancroft.berkeley.edu/Exhibits/MTP/index.html

The Mark Twain Papers & Project
http://bancroft.berkeley.edu/MTP

Mark Twain's Interactive Scrapbook
http://www.pbs.org/marktwain/scrapbook/index.html

Mark Twain's Mississippi
http://dig.lib.niu.edu/twain

PICTURE CREDITS

INDEX

Page numbers in *italics* indicate photos or illustrations.

ABOUT THE CONTRIBUTOR

LIZ SONNEBORN is a freelance writer living in Brooklyn, New York. A graduate of Swarthmore College, she is the author of more than 80 books for children and adults, many of which deal with nineteenth-century American history. Her works include *The American West*, *The California Gold Rush*, *The Mexican-American War*, *The Mormon Trail*, and *The Acquisition of Florida*. She has also written biographies of Harriet Beecher Stowe, Guglielmo Marconi, Will Rogers, Clara Barton, Samuel de Champlain, John Paul Jones, and Benedict Arnold.